Shearsman

double issue

79 & 80

Spring / Summer
2009

Edited by
Tony Frazer

This issue of *Shearsman* magazine is published in the United Kingdom by
Shearsman Books Ltd
58 Velwell Road
Exeter EX4 4LD

www. shearsman. com

ISBN 978-1-84861-023-1
ISSN 0260-8049

Acknowledgements:
The translations of Norbert Hummelt are of poems from the volume *Totentanz*
copyright © 2007 Luchterhand Literaturverlag GmbH, Munich, and are printed
here by permission of the publisher. The translations of Hendrik Jackson are
of poems from the volume *Dunkelströme*, copyright © 2007, Kookbooks Verlag,
Idstein, and are printed here by permission of the publisher. The translations
of Antônio Moura are drawn from the volume *Rio Silêncio* (Lumme Editor, São
Paulo, 2004) and are printed here by permission of the publisher.

Subscriptions and single copies:
Back issues, from issue 1 to 62, may be had for £3 each direct from the press.
Subsequent issues—which are uniform with this issue—cost £8.50/$13.50
through trade channels. Single copies can be ordered for £8.50, post-
free, direct from the press, or from bookstores in the UK and the USA.
A subscription—covering two double-issues, each of 108 pages, costs £12
in the UK, £14 for the rest of Europe, including Ireland, and £15 for the
rest of the world. Longer subscriptions may be had for a proportionately
higher payment, which will insulate purchasers from further price-rises
during the term of the subscription. Those wishing to pay by credit card
may purchase individual issues from 63 onwards through the Shearsman
online store, accessible via www.shearsman.com.

Submissions
Shearsman operates a submissions-window system, whereby submissions
are only considered during the months of March and September,
when selections are made for the October and April issues respectively.
Submissions may be sent by mail or email, but email attachments—other
than PDFs—are not accepted. We aim to respond within 2 months of the
window's closure.

CONTENTS

Alan Wall	4
Anna Reckin	14
Robert Saxton	17
Kelvin Corcoran	19
Helen Lopez	27
Stefan Tobler	32
K.C. Clapham	34
Alasdair Paterson	37
Sarah-Anne Cox	40
Nick Potamitis	42
Catherine Hales	48
Nathan Thompson	51
Jen Crawford	55
Peter Robinson	57
Tony Williams	61
Lynne Hjelmgaard	68
Steve Spence	71
Michael Ayres	74
Norman Jope	79

Norbert Hummelt	82
Hendrik Jackson	86
both translated from German by Catherine Hales	
Óscar Curieses	91
translated from Spanish by Valentino Gianuzzi	
Melih Cevdet Anday	93
Özdemir Asaf	96
both translated from Turkish by George Messo	
Edoardo Sanguineti	100
translated from Italian by Ian Seed	
Antônio Moura	104
translated from Portuguese by Stefan Tobler	

Biographical Notes	106

Alan Wall

Ruskin and Sesame

> '. . . acting not as wealth, but (for we ought
> to have a correspondent term) as 'illth',
> causing various devastation and trouble
> around them . . .'
>
> John Ruskin, *Unto This Last*, 1860.

I

Like the man who, given radium
(A curio, a little gift, a tiny elemental)
Wore it on a silver string around his neck
And pointed out with pride this rarity
To all and sundry
Until it killed him,
Ruskin wore the rancour that he felt
For the grand machinery of fate
Turning its wheels inexorably in England;
For children working fifteen hours a day;
For ugliness emblazoned everywhere in iron;
Effie's faithlessness and Millais' malice.

Illth, he said. Written first then uttered
Before attendant crowds in lecture halls.
Illth. A moth clings to the syllable's end
Chewing holes in a gorgeous brocade
Riddled through with silk and golden thread
The length of a palace wall:
'NO WEALTH BUT LIFE.'
Illth. Furred fog of a word
Swallowing its mess of shadows
A soft-shoe-shuffle, a blur.
Bright wings mimic the rainbow
Only to sizzle in candle flame,
Such a tiny sun to die in.
There's illth.
When insect heads explode in adoration

Of the incandescent gas
One exiguous wick provides.

II

The age was steaming up.
Outside his window, industry
Re-fashioned nature in its image,
But to whose advantage exactly?
Commodities are zeroes multiplying in a ledger-book.
In lecture after lecture, he demanded
'What is wealth? What illth?
'By our art and architecture, books, music
'We'll be known, should this our name survive at all
'The great entropic principle our age is formulating . . .'

Railways vein the land, and snorting engines
Heave their loads up gradients. Pig iron,
Rubble for roading, tin trinkets, coal.
Out of the earth's resources, its riches
We fashion our world.

III

Sessie looks up from her book. Her parents called her
Sesame in honour of Ruskin's *Sesame and Lilies*.
She sits in Soho and sees winter light
Falling through windows to meet
Dusty air, dirty carpets
Like an exhausted allegory, a Dutch painting:
17th Century, each itemised mundanity illuminated
As though saints' faces glowed at windows
Bright nuclei in the oval windows of their atoms.
Her gin and tonic has dissolved its ice.
Her profile is familiar in the gloom.
Stray drinkers shuffle to the bar
Like spoiled priests at a communion rail
Assessing how much faith remains to be exhausted.

Winter light.

What are we observing here, from such a distance?
A woman of a certain age and disposition
Whose breasts passed through the Bohemian
Hands of Soho
Like rations through the hands and mouths of hungry ratings
Whose thighs clutched
Torsos of painters
Sculptors, poets,
Drunks with no profession
But the Goddess Booze
A litany of foggy splendour
In veneration of befuddled dereliction.

She sees herself now as she once saw Nina Hamnett—
''Modigliani said I had the finest tits in Europe'—
Fading slowly with a glass before her
Waiting for the fellow from the BBC. Tristan.

Sesame Twilling, late child of the Twilling Shipping Line.
You will find her listed in the books as Cecil Twilling
With a note explaining how the name was really Cecilia.
But the name was really Sesame
Cut down in turn to Sessie.
She'd given up on the confusion years before
Becoming simply Cecil Twilling
For all official purposes. Why not?
(Some thought it the argot of an ancient dyke)
But to herself she was and always would be Sessie.
Now Sessie awaited Tristan.

Her semi-abstract paintings
Exhibited, reproduced, admired throughout the 50s
By Herbert Read, Ben Nicholson and Barbara Hepworth.
Francis had said nothing
In all the hours she'd spent with him at Muriel's
Staring into the eyes of one stone god or another
As the champagne pinked its bubbles

And words ballooned.
But Francis, she knew, thought little enough of anyone
Still living and holding a brush,
Apart from a few like Lucian and of course himself.
Even Jackson Pollock was no more than 'the lacemaker'
The dynamic threading of his drips condemning him
To the millinery section of a haberdasher's shop.

Sessie knew that she'd done something
Still could on certain days
When her hands weren't trembling
In her tiny attic studio in Highgate.
She'd had a fragment of the vision bequeathed her—
Few enough do, and she knew it.
So now she waited.
For Tristan from the BBC.
A third her age.
Who modelled his brain for the camera
As though this mind might strut nude and enticing,
A Plato lap-dancing before his avid patrons.

Illth. When a steam engine shouted
It used to make that sound
                            however briefly.

Illth illth illth. Right up the gradient
Towards the summit.

Ever onwards and upwards:
Her father, the shipping magnate
Sir Thomas had been keen on
Climbing every mountain.
He'd disinherited her at twenty-one
When word got back to Twilley House in Bucks
(His own armorial device on the gates,
A trifle gaudy, she'd always thought)
How many boho bucks had been riding the family maiden.
Ah, those were the days. Who needed eminence?
Give me back my body, Sessie thought.

My body, my verve, my bonding boys.
I came up with a strategy to deal with them:
Whenever they jumped me, I jumped right back.
Some stopped there and then
Astounded at such symmetrical relations between genders.

Ben Nicholson took Cubism and made it pastoral
Softened its diagrammatic edges
Transmuted it to English pastel and topography.

An alchemical process dependent on curious distillations
Afforded by the Cornish coast, climatic metamorphoses
A mathematical approach to nature
And the primitive panache of Alfred Wallis
Old sailor home from the sea
Filling his scraping boards with colour
Hearing the devil farting down his chimney every evening.
Ben looked and saw what art should be:
A spectrum of delight in nature, minus affectation.
Her own view entirely.
She spent two years down there in Cornwall with them
Even got taken one night by a poet in Zennor
In a field laid with frost while a motionless goat looked on.
Next day she was too hung-over to recall whether or not
She'd called out in pleasure. All she remembered
Was green and white, grass, frost, and that motionless goat
His eyes tiny beacons in the darkness
                    (vertical, verdant flares)
And a heroic fumbling through duffle and wool
                    and dark wooden buttons.
And where then is Tristan? Is he parting at last from Isolde?
Maybe they too are spreadeagled in a Cornish field.
That would explain the delay in getting started.

IV

Here is Ruskin on rust in Tunbridge Wells in 1858.

It's richer than gold, and a better provider
We could litanize
The life of metals with the breath put into them,
For the breath of life in Genesis is oxygen
As well as *ruah* or *pneuma*—
The ochreous stain on the marble is a form of beauty.
Your eyes should fill with salt each time you see
Iron in such a state of rust.

Only one metal which will not rust readily
And that has caused Death rather than Life;
It will not be put to its right use till it is made
A pavement of, and so trodden under foot.

The family gold had been denied to Sessie
Whatever coin she'd had she made herself.
Never a fashionable a painter, if greatly admired.
Now out of fashion entirely.

Coniston Water darkens
When the mood of the weather turns tragic
As though recalling how transient all things are
Including the atmosphere of one small blue-veined planet.
From the house at the lake's edge if you listen closely
             you will shortly hear a scream.

V

In 1819 the Reverend William Buckland was appointed
Oxford's first Professor of Geology.
His house, which Ruskin visited, contained his specimens
Many still alive. There you might hear the rumbling of the bear,
The jackal's hungry keening, and eat from a menu
Rare in Oxford at the time. Among the *plats du jour*:
Battered dormouse and a crocodile sautée.
All the while animals moaned, cried out
In steerage, as though they were still on the Ark
With a drowned world rolling in the dark beneath them.
Not as loud, though, as Rossetti's menagerie on Cheyne Walk

Where Swinburne and the monkeys out-gibbered
                    one another nightly
A mouth no more than an orifice for verbal defecation.
All these cries entered Ruskin's mind. Years later
In madness in Brantwood
                at the edge of Coniston Water
Such voices would be
Ventriloquised by Satan at a greater volume.

By then they wouldn't scare, those creatures from Saint Anthony's
Apocalypse. None of his screams could budge
His shape-shifting tormentors so much as an inch.

VI

Tristan arrives at last. A pretty boy, no doubt of that.
Did Nature do his hair
Or is coiffure required to put a little curl
                right in the middle of his forehead?
Years before she'd most likely have had him.
Years? Decades more like. And he's flirtatious too.
After twenty minutes with a camera hovering
                hither and thus
She realises with a thump that the programme is not really
About artists she knew,
Like Nicholson and Hepworth,
And their relation to her own life's work
As she'd been told (however vaguely)
In the phone-call.
But instead the theme is anecdote and gossip,
The usual suspects from Soho and Fitzrovia.
'I think I'd like another drink,' she says. 'A double.'
Tristan proffers his charm as though it should prove
Sustenance enough for any arty dowager.
Thus with his winsome smile:
'You only slept with Dylan once, I think, but you must have
Met him many times before and after.'
Ah yes, the Welsh boy, Celtic
Waves poured smoothly

Into a decanter of cut-glass BBC urbanity.
She could still remember vividly enough.
No distinction earned in sleeping once with Dylan;
More trouble not to.
She takes a steady drink and feels the gin break through.

'My name's not really Cecil.'
'Cecilia, isn't it?'
'No, Sesame, in fact. As in *Sesame and Lilies,* a work you know, I'm sure.
Why did Ruskin take to political economy, d'you think?
As odd, as troubling in its way as Ezra Pound adopting economics
For a theme. 1860. *Unto This Last.*
He even invented a word to try to describe the nightmare
We inhabit: illth. Not wealth but illth.
Now Soho when I knew it was an escape from illth.
We made no trinkets here, though a few
Sold their bodies— quite a bargain basement, this place.
When Ruskin ranted about
The Great Exhibition of 1851, all those commodities
Parading themselves under steel and glass
                    like tremulous bodies
All the gewgaws, the gimcrack pleasantries
Of mass production, while paintings were rotting
At that very moment in the rain in Venice
After the Austrian bombardments,
He was pointing us all to a future in Soho.
You will keep this in, won't you Tristan?'
(He nods and she knows he is lying).

'Here you see we only cared for what deserved our caring.
We painted, we wrote, made music, stole,
We didn't pay taxes, and yes, I grant you, young man,
Now and then we made love, but who doesn't? Your programme
Should try to explain how for half a mile around
These parts we fled the illth and tried to find true wealth
In one another's company, one another's paintings,
One another's arms.'

Later back at the BBC with a listless crew, Tristan shrugs
To his producer:
'Bugger all, I should think.
Old bint just kept banging on about Ruskin.'

VII

Sessie sits in the back of the taxi
Taking her to Highgate
And lifts from her bag
An olive-green volume
Published in 1891
By George Allen of Sunnyside, Orpington
And 8, Bell Yard, Temple Bar, London.
Sesame and Lilies by John Ruskin, LL.D.
Already the twelfth edition in the original form.
Inscribed thus: *To My Darling Sesame,*
When others ask why you weren't named more predictably—
Marigold perhaps or Daisy or Rose—
Show them this rarity of prose.

With all my love, Father.

Sir Thomas. How she would like to meet him again now.
But then maybe she'd do that, shortly.

When she climbs unsteadily from the cab
She pays first, tipping too heavily
Then holds the book up to the driver's face.
'I was born inside that, you know.'

'Good for you, love. Take care up them stairs now.'

She wished Henrietta were still around.
Sessie would have said, 'All I wanted
Was to talk about my work,
While I still have a tongue in my head forming words.
All he wanted was to talk about
The size of Dylan Thomas's todger.'

Henrietta would have roared, as she frequently did
And poured them both another massive drink.

She lay on the bed and looked around her
At her paintings on the wall.
They were good, all of them. She knew that.
She couldn't have lived with them otherwise.

Ruskin's bed in Brantwood was surrounded
By Turner prints
Which hallucinated come night-time
Into demons shrieking.
Henrietta would have calmed him down
Pressing his head to her breast
(she bore little resemblance to Rose la Touche
as Bacon's *Reclining Nude With a Syringe*
or Deakin's porno shots make clear—
No anorexic, she).

'Poor Johnny,' she'd have said. 'Poor John.'

Sessie switches on the tiny television in the corner.
A black man and a white man chatting.
'How come you guys can sing so high when it suits you?'
'Must be all those centuries of white guys
Kicking us in the balls, man.'
'So that would explain your total lack of interest in sex
These days then, Harry.'
The laughter continues as she switches off the set.

And in the dark that night an engine panting
Illth illth illth
Is climbing its way to Coniston Water
Where the fish have already stopped dreaming.
An old man with hoarfrost on his head
And a Gothic rib-cage
Crouching naked in the corner of his room
Falls silent at last.

Anna Reckin

St Peter's, Castle Hill, Cambridge

Well in a grove

of thunder, in

a round yard

A line of limes up to the door, but what I remember are the cloudy
shapes of the branches of the hawthorn tree

X-tied now, lest

sprung apart

And the square stone stillness inside

Fabric

dusk	shoulders	ivies	bride's
name-tag	hips	girdle	blossom
folding	*figured*	*forced*	*repeats*
[ ]	satin	tartan	
			poppets
		[parition	]

Manifestation

white makes the pattern

                      via quiet lanes

etched, or as decals

           different kinds of rays and arrangements of circles

                          or dark steps in a wet field

As if that way

Move in amongst, as if
that way
you could hear
these grave-
posts, groves of gums,
dots of tree-shade:

> stems to be lost and listening in,
> between 'here stands,' under
> stood-for's

set foot, and scatter
    stet
     – as if it could

Based on *Edge of the Trees*, an installation by Fiona Foley
and Janet Laurence at the Museum of Sydney

On Wicklow Fells

Argan Spraint, a shepherd's son, knew the constellations
before he knew the alphabet. One sheep, valiant against
predators, he named O'Ryan.

The fells of Wicklow teem with knitted sheep.
Our cottage mumbles in its cap of slate.
A stranger dances, gravely, on the grate.

The werewolf digs its den in human sleep.
A bear, with a grin, pours honey on the dawn,
your dewpond. A soot-speck fills your yawn.

The hills of Wicklow broil with ravelled sheep.
Some golf we played before our furze was burned.
Some gains we got before our lack was learned.

The Circulating Library

Two equine-equestrian pictures, with appended verse commentaries

For the dark riders of the spiritual frontier

Every night a dozen or so wild horses, souls of the wisest books, silently
move in towards the red-glowing ash-mound of the campfire, to drink from
quiet minds. Clouds know what rain knew once but can no longer remember.
Yet splashes they could never imagine, the raindrop's enlightenment,
a brilliant haiku in an epic of tedium. When the storyteller pauses mid-flow
for a punctuating silence, some endure suspense, while others, with relief,
hear the tale, its people, their pressures on our minds, and all the world
and all its winds, gallop off, thunderously at first, then quietening into
silence, swallowed into the living black centre of the wilderness where
horses gather, neigh greetings to each other, discover they can think,
and read, and speak, but need to find a better way to teach.

Cold starry night	*blackboard of night*
horses below	*chalk of snow*
their minds alight	*the true the trite*
with all they know	*and the cold rainbow.*

*

They linger still in our darkness, long after supper is over. We wonder
how they can help us, because surely they can, and wish to, surely.
They are like regrets, or in another mood the mistakes behind regrets,
or the uncertainties behind mistakes. Our understanding is to our sickness
as the weather is to our beloved valley—though many of us might imagine
the opposite. So precarious are our myths, a stallion can take the place of
a patriarch and be more intimate, on account of being a little less human.
The Muybridge file lies unopened in a forgotten corner of the mind. Gusto
is a wild cry, like 'Geronimo!' Acolytes occasionally take to the saddle,
not in the sacred shows, but galloping hard between monasteries,
carrying a thought before it has time to stiffen.

Wise is the animal	*that only thin air*
that needs no hands	*sustains its ride—*
and coming to a wall	*vaulting despair*
instantly understands	*to the other side.*

Byron's Karagiozis

This lake and town of Byron's escape
appears as fresh as a boy's face;
milord's playthings arrayed across the plain,
the shoreline stepping in and out of the ever living past.

The Pasha scans the mountain paths for rebels
rising to the blue of Ottoman heaven,
saunters along the landing strip of the unaligned
—my palace, my lands of blood, my lord—welcome.

We dropped out of thin air over the Pindhus,
a door opened became a flood of light;
landing gear scarring the face reflected
the water full of boats and sacked women.

This the first Albanian song of Lordy Viron,
the second a lamentation of unrequited love;
the clarinos sob sob, the real men howl
—ah your pink ears, their coral portal and lightshine.

*

Scene 1

Enter Spiridion Foresti, British Consul, dancing with the Governor of
    Malta,
cloaked in smiles—'We can send young Byron to traverse the province,
let him bind the Pasha by his vices to our cause, and just think
how well it will be received—an Albanian front against Napoleon.'

'Does the young lord have to know? Reputation says he's of the same kind,
he can be our Karagiozis, with a big fat cock to catch the devil.'
A paper boat bobs across the screen, the Spider, British warship, flags flying,
and off goes Byron to Prevesa, dumb little thing in a puppet show.

*

The music is different village to village,
in my village Konitsa, it is lighter, other places
sadder—like the stone we build black or white,
the stone is just for that village, the right stone.

But the songs, most songs, all over about the same,
being away, not home, songs of away, to say exile,
as they play for you, you know Saturday, off work,
the longing of Albania or another Greece or Germania.

*

Eleftheria showed us the painted Ottoman door
taken from the dump, under the blackened surface
a blue green meadow of flowers and birds interwoven
flooding a lattice of apricots and pinks.

Idealised peony or rose, an eternal spring at the centre
the habitation of songbirds, rescued from the tip,
—we keep it here, not in our rooms, so all can see
and the colours of the house are taken from it.

*

From the capital of the East
two experimental cantos,
the minarets of Tepelene like meteorites
—who now shall lead the scattered children forth?

Journey made difficult by Ramadan and rain
nine hours lost in the storm at Zitza,
we lit fires, fired guns to find the party;
Byron, cloaked to his eyes, under a rock, content.

Remembered lowering coast and the name—Missolonghi,
dark mind on darker waters held silent;
Wahhabi's rebel brood, their pious spoil
a path of blood running to the west.

At Ioanina the houses and domes
glitter through gardens of lemon and orange trees,
the lake spreads itself from the cypress grove
making a track into a land of no fixed boundaries.

★

Scene 2

At the Karagiozis staged for Ramadan, Hobhouse and Byron agog;
on the other side of the art of the theatre of shadows
Captain Leake unloads guns and ammunition,
Ali Pasha enters, raises his eyebrows and pats the ordinance.

Byron skips on in Albanian finery, begins a letter—My Dear Mother,
he reveals to the audience an enormous penis strung from his neck;
straining, he soliloquises and beats the beast, rolling across the floor,
admiring his guest's performance, eyes alight, the Pasha approaches.

★

The stone villages rise and fall
as if abandoned on rolling Zagori,
we saw photographs of children
on the walls of all the tavernas.

Formal, dressed in white
for a festival in the platea,
rows and rows of children
from fifty years ago.

★

You must be quiet crossing the bridge,
stop the music, dismount and step softly.

Don't let the one sacrificed below
catch us at our wedding in this upper world.

If she hears the music she'll join the party,
the bridge collapse and we'll never cross over.

★

Scene 3

A large room paved with marble, a fountain playing at the centre, men lounge
and suck sherbet; then to a rough fanfare painted boys in spinning circles sing
'Oh your curling hair and small ears.'—Ali, ornate craft borne aloft by many hands,
responds profundo, 'You must think of me as a father, a father, a father.'

As the tide of seduction rises with pretty animals, sweetmeats and aerial Ali,
the devil descends and affixes the monster penis to the image of every future
lover, mistress, wife and sister of the alarmed poet: Byron darkens
and grits his teeth, smoke from his burnt journals obscures the scene.

★

Streets dark all day, damp
tip tap from the dance school,
houses slumped in glutinous air
nothing for it but drown in the lake.

I am sick of vice, tried all its varieties,
it's time to leave off wine and carnal company
and betake myself to politics and decorum;
—a vast mountain that little word.

Then from the bazaar a wedding party dances,
her hat of gold coins, her face painted red and white,
the men singing—Erotica Erotica, a sweet song for ladies
echoes off the whole world, the girl in coins glinting.

Looking at you what language is left?

The passes we travelled have left a river running in my heart.

The dragomen were silent crossing the bridges.

In that small bay Antony lost the world.

*

The Albanian girls circle the square
on bikes borrowed from the Ingalish,
—thank you, thank you, we bring back,
silver spokes turning spindly legs push.

They circle under the tower's long shadow
and the day darkens for time to stop,
the mountains come falling down falling down
and the world walks away on terraced light.

*

Scene 4

On this side of the art of the theatre of shadows
Ali Pasha is beheaded by his Ottoman masters in 1822,
the blue and white flags of a new nation flood the land
and Byron, poster boy in exile, would lead the children forth.

*

By morning we woke in the bowl of mountains,
snowbound peaks shining up the sky chemicals
of the big fat day on its feet and shouting.

The clarino rising wails—what word, what root will break
the rock wolves in rounds, heads back sing, pelts spark
black Zagori night unveils the first light of another country.

23

Reading *The Cantos*

1

Fell asleep in the courtyard reading *The Cantos*
after swimming rolled on white waves and ankle stones,
Malatesta and the Magnificent, the bloody mechanics.

After the dazzling verse and magnetic names
I remembered two hours sat before the girl Aphrodite,
the intermittent light and the crowd parting occasionally.

Her hair lifts, she dreams the name of a new world,
the sea surrounds us on all sides and the light
comes and goes over her meadows and pathways.

What does Pound find to admire in Sigismundo and the Medici?
Hands grasping the rods of power, banking and patronage,
polishing the azure air for the faces of Tuscan gods?

I woke up in cherry season, ate the cherries ripe and wet,
the sea breathing in the olive groves, clouds rising from the hills,
to see ants hoist crumbs to a depthless sky.

2

The wind cases the house all night
rolls away to reveal the harbour washed
the sea lanes rise and fall.

How grand to propound the big idea;
interest rates as rented money
made all art go rotten after 1527.

A species of modernist ambition
to synthesise the culture's cache,
a gesture, anti-Semitic and parochial.

The wind cases the house at night
to reveal the coastline hung out to dry,
Europe and the Faithful heard on the air.

Chanting of dumb beasts sanctioned
their reasoning is shallow
they speak to popular prejudice.

Small birds drill the sky in an agony
of Spring it is it is it is the force of them,
they sing song a theology of awake.

The merchants of the Morea carried
the sprouting branch and sharp mind
where she sets her foot to the sea.

What nerve they had to outstare
Mehthoni and Corroni, eyes of
the serene empire's trade routes.

Platsa, above us on the mountain, traded
directly with Venice on donkeys, down
the calderimi to the harbour of the world.

3

And then in Canto XLIX his genius
breaks your heart, imperial power is
what is it?—the rushing particles ignite.

The little owl glides to its shadow
high on the wall of the broken tower
above the middle sea that makes us.

The widow walks across the square
she is not long a widow, she is a black line
carrying road-side flowers to her neighbour.

Turning the dynamo Cadmus turned
Euratos rises on the running wave
Europa of wide open eyes steps ashore.

Everywhere
                    scattered song
the host
            a fishing boat draws the west skyline

Dead Dogs

The problem with big space projects is that there are fewer national
caveats failing to meet objectives. Stripped of responsibilities, chess
board killers offer dead dogs drinks for want of temperate language.
The risk to the public is quite small if one claps at the end of a video
conference. 14 poppy free provinces but NATO could do better. The
soul makes guns go off—a tick box for isolating the extremist. In the
garden after lunch where the bougainvillea rains, I shall water
the saladini both fresh and weary.
If you lower your voice you can defeat
her screams as another rebel group withdraws. The unhappy
Secretary General is staying the course
'no fast exit' shielded again by temperate language.

Boxing in the Pipes

"Lot 555 white ceramic vases—no,
in the skip they go." The advantages of having a project manager who
buys one and gets one free is that they are much more in keeping with
condiments close at hand. "An oriental blue and white charger 10, 5-
anyone? 2, 2 I'm bid, 4, 4 bid . . ." Ideas to steal for an organised larder
in New England style tradition—dream kitchen. ". . . 6 bid, 6 should
be double that, lovely for the Christmas table..." He always thought
painted units were a good idea until gutting and remodelling went out
of fashion. ". . . 6 sold and away, 114, quality lot that. Zenith 35mm
Camera Lot 561, 2 on the camera, 2 pound on him, sold and away at 2
pound, err I'll take 3, 5, 7 I'm bid, all out sir, ladies bid on my right, 9, 9
and off." In the new extension there is room for an extra table and tree
at Christmas and even in winter it feels like summer.

Permit

Tensions are
palpable and
the law has
made fools
of us all
putting public
safety at risk.
What went
wrong? He
texted a friend
and London
on a heightened
state of alert
let shooting
an innocent
become a
breach of
health and
safety.
Commander
control lost
the strapline
and had no
idea the
radios didn't
work underground.
Major failings,
serious and
avoidable errors
meant the
implementation of
order to stop
was preceded by
shoot on sight.

A Time to Shine

1. Rise Above

Start up by nurturing success, aim high steal ideas, net work. This is real time research by the experts roaming the room in a culture of enterprise and a living system with flexible funding solutions. This is a time to shine the net effects on the stock of geographic indicators, dynamic and innovative processes in place with a clear mandate for leadership. This snapshot will inform policy and decide the churn rate of team breakdown. This paints a vision for the future on an economic development canvas, stretched and ready to boomerang straight back the trends in the right direction. It is service to say that with our foot on the gas our geography is an asset. 3 hubs in our engine room manage and lead space, skills and strands. Fleet of foot and with a single slide we operate in a vacuum of heavy manufacturing.

2. Uncommon Results

The gross added value sustaining the community in physical spaces has processes in place for project failure that shape the retail and leisure hub. A footfall comes in as a positive lever in the public sector, and in the right time frame we could have a symbiotic relationship. The trick there and here, in a winter wonderland is to maximise the benefits of eco prioritisation in a global Christmas market. Clever knowledge industries manage and lead the spirit of partnership with the right solutions going forward. Light composite materials spend alone and give up sovereignty for the greater good. Clever stuff - creative industries, a prize winning local supplier, distinctive and unique along the costal strip we have the sea. The time is right for small and medium sized leisure opportunities, businesses that will endure and shine.

3. What's In It for Me?

When you set out goals and activities for the year break into your creativity. Brainstorm your thought shower. "You are always only 12ft from an opportunity" Look back on your life with 20/20 vision, manage your memories and then lay them to rest. Mainstream the diversity contractor with key icons, opportunities come hidden, camouflaged and sometimes on a plate. Seize and be aware of the abundance theory in hindsight develop your sagacity, try more little and often and discover the habit of flipping the negative. Only visit with pit stop pessimisms. Bounce back fuelled by meaning. Go the extra yard and mexican wave your future by living and breathing the bigger picture. Define your elephant thick skin with your yes/no quota and connect with others. Multiplicity in action and disruptive thinking make good quality conversation when you need to get going.

4. In Good Stead

Be the best you already are—your future your choice. The science of rapport has a formula for success. There you go, wherever you are. Even at a visioning meeting navigate your dreams with a search engine for charisma. This is root canal surgery for fear and don't forget to bring passion to work with you. You will get what you always get if you do what you always do. Discount the future cash streams with highly desirable phases of travel. The absolute grail is a big step forward that clarifies the concept and hugs people. Focus above the hurdles, seek approval and the project will champion clout. Smart goals have beautiful outcomes. The mission statement has specific hidden agendas that lifestyle your leadership gurus with a contingency plan.

5. Breakout Session

How do you know what you have got at the end of the day? A novel set of interrelated activities that trade off each other until their end performance. Tot them up for the bottom line and domesticate the logic because this is a complicated network of dependency. For what it is worth phase and lay against the calendar the point of no return where ideas ought to be chasing the money. Expand the lift efficiency of current capacity, monitoring and controlling the completion handover sign off. A logical sequence of tracked events and operations are ultimately closed down.

Bearer Bound

She banked her head in a paintless mess,
a real fear that deals in nutshells on a

standard night. Light walks through, timeless, and it is now what she

thought it was. The truth is cyclical weakness and high confidence at the

same time. We wake up and today it is not the case, it can't happen
      and left alone

we fall in, slowing or pushed we stretch
a fraction, talk and fret a bit.

Mechanism

Monarchs use the sun as a compass to guide them on their 2000 mile
round trip booking a holiday is a great way of beating the post-Christmas
blues the key gene CRY2 identified in the monarch butterfly that acts as a
biological clock for estimating the 24-hour cycle of the circadian rhythm
because Britons (even in a credit squeeze) are far more likely to cut
down on the big ticket items and luxury consumer goods than on their
beloved holidays cryptochrome—a light sensitive protein which counts
the passing hours of each day and also communicates the information
to the monarch's inbuilt solar compass for the insect to calculate its
correct direction of flight the appallingly wet summer last year will
encourage more of us to head abroad and swap the UK's unpredictable
climate for guaranteed sunshine we have still to understand how the
tiny brain of the Monarch butterfly which is no bigger than the head
of a ball point pen can arrange information about time and space that
leads it to carry out the appropriate flight behaviour.

Stefan Tobler

Canción

1.
Each body with its desires
and the air carries sea-salt

two bodies share a bed
and the sea between them

the old song on the radio
the one they would fall asleep to

is the rhythm of a body
and each body asks after its rhythm

each body stopped and listening
and the song breaking each

lying next to the other
each facing the sea

2.
In plastic buckets
each carries with care
to bring for the other
what they can of the sea.

Note: the 'Canción' heard here uses a couple of lines from the Venezuelan poet Eugenio Montejo's poem of the same name.

[untitled]

Considering calmly, impartially,
this new machine to see with, and reading in its manual
that man or woman is nothing more
than composed of rectangles, ratios,
is a mutable mammal who combs
afterwards in PhotoShop, considering this camera
and the six paths of rightness on its settings dial
thunder runner mountain flower face heart,
and considering that we are sad animals,
cough and spit better than incited cats
but otherwise have little to endear us,
that our tongues have lost their honey
and that love would have room
to shelter in our mouths as it did
before I lost our cleaning rota and all hope,
and finding my eyes can't quite focus,
and nothing working quite, can I turn back
to the heart, and love, the mode for beginners,
just a click away, all I need
in most any light?

Note: This uses some phrases from an Antônio Moura poem, that are in turn half-taken from a Cesar Vallejo poem with a similar title, 'Considerando en frío, imparcialmente'.

K.C. Clapham

The List

1.   and I'm sitting down to write the list
      of things to write poetry about
      and it seems there are too many things
      to write in a list but not in a poem
      where one word can mean so much
      more than it does in prose and why
      not prose if it is no more; but the list,
      so, it should matter to me if it is in the list
      though to not matter is also a thing so
      that could be on the list and like anything
      because what doesn't matter: the list doesn't
      know, it is not a poem it does not matter
      but it could, to escape the list and become
      the poem is to matter, no matter the thing
      but it turns out the list has poetry written
      all over it and inside it, wrapped in poetry and
      it is listed, bookended, by that thing inside
      and out, if it seemed wrong to waste ink,
      to waste time to the arrival of the princess, towing
      a cloak of heavy words that now were
      right to be listed because here they are;
      though the list became questions that answered me
      back up the list and it shifted and turned against me,
      attacking me with its listless questions and I had no
      answers—why wasn't it on the list, why were notes
      connected and why had the gun pointed the bullet
      back into the list

2.

I swear there were no shadows in China Town,
to hide me between trees and the notebook.
And 'China Town' is a junk, boating rubbish recycled
from the vast stream of chatter that I like to remember
with a pen, in a note in the book. Note. Add to list. Note to note,
start escape plan.

Wolf

and the woodcutter began to cut open the wolf.
He began with the W, it was coarse and familiar
like his own hands. My My Wolf, what a furry
distraction you have.

The O peeled away like a rubber glove inside out.
All the better to see your insides with, it was a
library of tiny texts, tiled fast. The discarded
was a beast itself.

Red Riding Hood and Grandma crawled out of
all that was still there and walked off. L was
inside the wolf cave, a fibre woven into a wall
the woodcutter halved.

F was still inside the wolf when they filled him with
rocks. A whole shape with new weight; the woodcutter's
wolf-shape would hide between different trees and move
in new forestry.

The Pawn Shop

        I am always facing the shelves.

        They are filled with space

    rockets and library building

    blocks towering over mountains of history

    books and springs of summer

    rain drops like a brick

through the windows the whole displays

every thing in side all at one view to focus

on and under all things one above all things.

I am struck by the effacing shelves

they shower with shells beached

with binary encoding the sky shelved

      waiting for a pocket in the party—always busy else where

the flies snaking to fly off to a sentence

                some years a moment

        The shop shelves
        numbers keys letters stamps marks

    made to order

no thing fits in boxes everything   squeezes

The both shelved and spare
—simultaneous— for ever   —simultaneous— for ever

the boats

   dock stationary

cutting through

seas

they leave and arrive appearing expected and surprising always meaning past the shelves leaning forward stretching back past foundations sailing from space to passage filling and clearing ways shipping data cargo weighted with the world shelved elements—the material fires of the words burning in space.

from On the Governing of Empires

On fire

lightning shimmy   lucifer scratch   liberated spark   libertine smoulder

leaf spasm   licked spruce   lemontree squeeze   lilac spurt

lacewing shrivel   lizard stencil   leveret skirl   lark suttee

luminous stable   lantern stairwell library smokehouse   lighthouse steeple

lake sanctuary   larch survivor   lung sfumato   lurking sequel

On heresy

stars come solitaries first
then a host like
pilgrims no crusaders

this rock that bleached
all day in the sun
still isn't white enough

do you prefer
the desert places or
the cities of the plain
I like best the view
of lights from up here

a breath of rosemary
perfection in the air
but the bridge is the devil's

On optics

reading from the top
it's down there they
broke the glass
burned the books
and their true believers
or reasonably similar
or just different

last lines are
the streets shone
then it was darker

On psyche

underneath all of it

fountains and roses
silk weave and moths
morgues birthing chambers
perfumed kisses dripping
clocks and tortures

under all the names
for the gods and their
mouths that can't be parched
for fear of uncomfortable silences

under all of it
you're into the vast
cisterns built for long siege
dim light on amber surfaces
slime and sleek byzantine carp
pillars from unseen to unseen

and round a corner
to stop you in your tracks
head of great medusa

On tragedy

out in the drenched unseen
was where the worst
usually came to the best
colonnades are what you think
but colonnades were just
the metrics and a long
echo till the building failed

by then the gods had shut up shop
slipped the search parties
bought gash papers laid low
reopened in the workshop zone
and there they took their long breaks
in the courtyard of chestnut flambeaux
or under a naked storeroom bulb
pointing the workclothes at
a chorus of death masks
and torsos pockmarked with the years
banging on about an upturn as if

nemesis meantime was no
longer the death of the past
no scarcely to be recognised in her
new uptown solo business set-up
focussed and going for volume
and hell if some customers
missed the personal touch
there was no denying
the groaning indexed shelves
those great marketplace stats

Sarah Anne Cox

from Truancy

search and research finally
under the library heading "problem children"
the frame of what is offered, expected
problemkinder, cross culturally rotted
Jon was a boy who had magic

Jon was a boy who had magic
was the beginning of his story
the one he was writing
the one constructed of hope
a fine line drawing
the first line
of course life will be what you make it
of course, meritocracy
and the good clarity of addition and subtraction
a correct answer filling in for wonder
a battery of psychological inquiries
I have seen the smoking man before
in a green tattered copy of Othello
on folded up Latin homework

For some people
that we do the same thing
is important
we string the wooden primary beads
go not straight to walking, but crawl first
go to school
sleep alone

For some people
implication runs backwards and sideways
for instance, a binder titled
"Daily Behavior Rating"
In the front office desk
some children biting or
weeping go into this book

For some people the number
3 can point right or left
for some, the r is a w in sound

I has never been the same as you

Nick Potamitis

---

nine coffins : a masque for nectanebo

1.

a poem, abstract'd from the royal bedroom

is more, perhaps, than blowsy tsifteteli, or
razor'd statements filling green refuse-sacks

by the road . with these computers can make

an assemblage . behold, a pale dust-cart
bent on waking the dead & neither must you
write down your mother's maidenhood,

the din / such delicate matter . those clamorous

bin-jockeys up at dawn to claim our midden-
heaps—a blight'd wreath—that rowdy
parataxis . by hand, re-program'd refuseniks
will need a bit under six-hundred years

doing the job (for chri'sakes) it's damn
too early for that racket, pantokratoras .

2

careening past brassy roma at the platform,

your man & his massive sunglasses disappear
beneath the train . the marble king is asleep .

the man with sunglasses might be an actor

in the part of man falling under a train,
a necessary geometry of position . no one
ever dies, everyone is always already dead,

the tally—on war footing ready to mobilise

—is zero, zero, one & still the marble king
sleeps . that same man, haul'd so many yards,
now a human accordion, his moody pass-
port reads bricoleur balkan nektanebos (

an outstretch'd hand / the sleeping stones
) give them a turn on your squeezebox .

3

nightmare outbreak of violent chicken's disease

with pictures . nightmare cowl'd gangs
in the forecourt are a real nightmare, a not

very dada suicide on the metro . consider

how she loves muscley arms, stakes out –
for future reference—her cleo from five till
seven bed-chamber, wounding & immaculate

as the wings of swans . indifferent, the swan

is a presence in the poem even if poland makes
more ready for nightmare war (one shorn
clean at the shoulder joint / parts of shoulder
bone scatter'd recalling tube mice) & always

on a promise, she would let him only when
he wore that nightmarish ram's head mask .

4

bandwidth & roving 'gyptians are stain'd by grief

the same as linen garments—damn'd / the damages
– his meat thought at no loss, with neat hand only

. things fit together . a basement gallery-space

if she can get away, mojitos, talk of graffiti-
inflect'd art well-hung . two inconsequential
things will fit together, become a consequence

(cropping his beard, his head shaven) mis-

taking her & by her mistaken . as ever, with all
eastern warfare, when the king retreats the buffer
overflows collapsing memory stacks . like small
wax ships on a bronze basin of rain-water,

a poem says jack, is never by itself alone . time
is a concrete continuum quotes jill, in repose .

5

theft is always analogous to mathematical

procedures . there are always remainders .
inspector n.tannenbaum's roving warrant

from pelusium to macedonian pella via the rail-

ways' police semantic web . what's left is the
set of these good / bad objects, the queen—
her sick body—mendoza the jew's bent elbow

& that schoolboy winning every marble .

a function, mon cher juve, of the man vaulting
an automatic ticket barrier . a secret platonic
dossier probably does exist . well-order'd,
it consists of statements given (in a dream

about warring factions) my arms are lost –
they approach me—this fast-track truncation .

6

the perseverence of birds over the mountain,

of the poem-computer's royally amorous intrusion .
topology tells us, each element is an equivalence,

symbolic—mostly of real hurt—somewhere

between gods & butchers . the elements being
grammatically uncertain (this ill-conditioning)
precarious as rum nizhinsky resonant with threat

. let the burn mark on her wrist serve for the real

ryght-arm'd in heart, he did hym downe to the
dytch—knock'd spark-out for filching documenta,
or haw-hawing the wrong faces . other versions
have the poem-computer for pseudo-callisthenes

—that need to provoke a stupid embroilment
again—so much ache / so much belly-aching .

7

a zakopane night-train & from the bottle

niña drinking her home-brought bulgarian
red . niña is a character in a different poem .

more healthy than gin, she stands here for

amplification / for generic processes &
previous war damage . a footnote is a footnote
is a fat clever crow sings jon in warszawa,

gamely wearing his song & dance-man's hat

. niña is (not) that balkan starlet famously
a young royal in dupin contra fantômas .
let's say—by affective peer-review—she
really does marry assistant conductor witold

nectanebosz, falling hard in a stand-up row
over corkage . let's say there are resonances .

8

the angel of silence taken wing . rouse

yourself old man, wake-up, go tell them
you play the better violin . ravens are military

spy-planes, would say a poem should be a lusty

noise, must croak like a frog smoking dog-ends .
& truly, he is not yet risen—strategically –
his word lent support by that wide-awake

suit, dapper log-book of his observances (with-

out interpretation) no space here for proper
french manners, just reconnoitring . the angel
having flown, leaves birds to pry, left our
lady's creaky ikon . rouse-up, king of the rom

& remember, beneath her vestments a large
candle she raises / it went aflame .

9

would you hit a woman with a child ? vulture-

wing'd like a polish lancer, return'd general
james & a makriyanni shoe-black barrack'd

as one by ox-flaying sleet—her split plastic bag

—all elements of the set of disavow'd elements .
the poem-computer is not for conflict resolution,
nor is zeus-under-the-ground, suffers phlegm

& the consequences of phlegm, us (the lost ones

) unwrit in the catalogue of the world, spilling
discount'd viscera & only our impotent
inspector—toothless chewer of corpses—to
clutch an exhibition fighter's plaster arm & cuff

copper-bound nectanebo's fallen limb / a lap-
top / the poem, singing not me, i'd use a brick .

Catherine Hales

six sonnets

who writes that sort of thing by hand any more
it's a short step from that to putting it all aside
for a pocketful of buy two get one free & who
can say whether this is just incompetence
or the result of a well-thought-out strategy
the subtext being as it's always been an improvement
on last year's menu & improvisation as a means
of placing hand on heart & aching for authentic
melodrama complete with mandolins
& all the trimmings the offer stands please
read carefully it's wholly inappropriate
a crispy base just like in the restaurant
I'm not sure where all this is leading but I like
the punctuation you may tick more than one box

we'd expected a few hold-ups but nothing like
this choke of traffic backed up to the border
it's not all doom & gloom you know & breaking
news & palimpsests & clearing misconceptions
the air-conditioning on the blink & then
the lack of running water we didn't deserve
where can we put our trust if not in the power
of broken stones plaintive spaces & public
declarations we apologise for any in
convenience due to disruptions to services moving
forward we set our goals high we're setting standards
in quality & price judge us by our results
for account information please press one for your
security this conversation is being recorded

arterial infractions spillage of imagining
what you look like after hearing your voice
on the radio the houses collapsed into a hole
in the ground medieval chalk pits no-one knew
were there they weren't marked on any map we
were plonked down in the middle of nowhere & told
to find our own way back some were never
heard from again multiple fractures &
concussion & there were people taking pictures
even before the police & ambulance arrived
they listen to the frequencies how toxic
well we wouldn't want it getting into the ground
water white noise after five hours both carriage
ways cleared diversion ahead get in lane

the lines are made to work hard & yet
are totally imaginary stepping off the boat
& handing my coin to the ferryman I realise
that this isn't where I want to be at all
& the ferryman's refusing to take me back imagine
things really having the thick black outline we draw
them with to define contain divide & own
without recourse to the usual methodologies
the courts overstretched & it'll take several months
even to get a hearing the improbability drive
cranked up to maximum there's some poor bugger
outside the door says he's been summonsed doesn't
have a clue what he's supposed to have done the portrait's
cleverly painted the eyes follow you wherever you go

condition stable   since we know
our narrators can't be trusted
in fact they wobble quite a lot & that's
today in a crowded market at the busiest
proposals for an international ban on
respectively the manner of its conception
reported heavier-than-expected second-quarter
it was only afterwards that she   came down
in a residential area in the suburbs   our
preliminary analysis is confirming that
could be applied to producing   documents
left on a train   the forgery was undetectable
except for the age of the paper   a ridge of high
necessities of waiting   continuing fine

the wilful savaging of string quartets when
was the last time ice formed over the lakes
& even in august you'd be surprised prime
numbers are the key of course & prime
time tv the place for maximum exposure
unearthings of artefacts & fragments the ruined faces
of card players in a painting & ships that foundered
on rocks on the scillies thinking they were some-
where else entirely & hence the need for a method
for determining longitude down by the canal
people playing boules wasps crawling into
coffee cups you're not recording this are you
this is off the record mostly harmless though there are
trouble spots syntax integral to an understanding of

a haunting

before you enter   consider everything
    the difficulties inherent in 'belief'
she comes in   him too   we sit together
while the wheel goes round   put in your pennies
this one's on me
                    if you knew how to
would you lift the lid   expose the trick   know
goodness in removing the vestige of
    these thoughts   will you be returning   'dove-like'
if so/not sit here with me   you seem restless
keen to get on   is this right   well   it's
    soon this will I think concern me   how to
become more definite   outside your welcome
I prefer things like this   we discuss why
your thumb flickers nervously over the door

The Floating World

Here,
stroking the swing and fall of words,
the fishermen are patient,

for in the red chamber
the emperor's fat wife
limps in the shade,
her hand a sphere of light.

The emperor weeps for his ornate geographies
to the end of everything,
as if the lettering
'a corridor of locked doors'
paints watercolours in the afternoon.

Out among
is for gathering flowers –
new reds and blues, say:

Master of the embroidered foliage,
the windows of the libraries
fish in ancient pools

but patiently.
The laws of supply and demand
leave behind words that climb,
leave tawdry quays:
how the room fills with dried flowers
of the stars.

The emperor claims:
"In here I keep all,
trying valiantly not to move."

Outside, beyond the drizzle
clouds break on cliff faces.
They hover by the lolling bells,
deep and steady
in the quietness of thresholds.

A knock comes to the door,

and ahead,
surprised by swords and bones,
feathers and skin are cold to the touch.

"Her goodbye is the distance you colour yourself,"
he says,   while the sun   still for years
moves unmistakable for a moment.

Source: one line from each poem in
Alasdair Paterson's 'The Floating World'

beachcombing

talk warbling in cast iron
a small round painting on the beach
catching the polished surface

your patient with her crutch searches
for gold among the broken ormers
settling like stained glass

(after the foregoing remarks
it is perhaps necessary to state
that care should be taken in matters of taxation)

her advantage is to appeal
at the time and place of the meeting
(a printed form is provided for this purpose)

no harm done   the sea below
'the distance'   as if a landscape
these surfaces   they shake in your hand

the day through

the question is
                 when the tanks arrive
these are grand events   delinquent and mobile
in the upper left margin   the motif 'probability'

who is weeping in the lamplight 'all profits
go to the orphanage'   across the window
the rain sews silk and catches

take off your clothes

we try to be friendly without elite sexual references

the time is   or was

beside the skin of you
the bedding inches further   a
slender legacy of the lamp   orange warm
carried silently about the ward
linking arms and cracking under closed doors
affectedly

out is   bullet points   further down the stave
drying under the conductor's eager fingers
a thief caught without any hands   'what do you do?'

we are trying excessively not to react
the pill-box untouched on your bedside table
engraved with somebody else's initials

the delay between your fingers beginning to drum

a child upstairs in the sunken building
sings as it was taught by the fires in distant
cocktail cabinets
                         'we used to have one of those
     a tea   yes   no milk   the way
it is in other countries'

the pictures we'd jump to if we could
moving the beat of sirens   exactly 'how'
you light a candle in the dark
until a face appears that curiously matches
what is imagined   inference sloping into the shadows
plucking courage not to say 'come with me'   settled in
shutting the door   watching the cracks   then as if waiting

cup vertigo

leads me in to the precipice on a blue rope night. an incline, dogs for
anticipants, hand in mane.

inside the well up my gills open the stairs dent the walls where they
brush their weight. quilly fingers gather the way in small wet beads.

dilate the harelip hall. the horse lays on its side for the ECG. enlarged
one side, atrophied the other, all around the photographs, muscles
fire in sequence, drawings of the patterns of the hooves' scar the
floorboards then score.

at this edge I call the meeting. the shadow minister in his cube extends
his leg above his head, touches his toe to the glass, we touch, toe
print to toe print. fog wax and wane. x-ray waves fray through water's
privacy the patterns on its face and his, what I've come to ask about.
the horizontal upright a 90 degree dissipation sniffing my scalp,
cupping my face. exposed beams swell.

which were a split valve, a quiet consultation. learning to waltz a
three-legged stool. in the 2/4 garden the rhinoceros. wore his horn.

Albumblatt

THERE IS A SLIMY LEAF ON A ROCK THE ARCH OF THE ROCK YOUR
MINDS BACK EXACTLY LIKE A WORM CASING INTO THE EARTH WHILE
EVERY SNAP-NECKED TREE A GOOSE DEAD SILLY ON THE GREAT

PLAIN DRIPS ITS FEATHERS COMPOSED OF CELLULOSE TUBES
COLLECTING IN THE FOG AT ONCE SLIPPERY AND SHIFTING LIGHT
THESE FUNCTIONS SO USEFUL AND DECIDEDLY A METAPHOR IS VERY

GOOD LIKE LITERATURE FOR THEORY ITS CHEST MAKING MY STEPS
EVEN AND MY CHEEK WET AS A MAN ON MY LEFT HIP PULLS SWING
FROM THE CHATELAINE HAIR DERIVES FROM THE FIT SNAKE CURL

viaduct

a reward, a hand on the back on the small of the back.
walking out to a car. a night, a tiredness, a whisper.
your tiredness and that you did well.
building a wall around it. like a harbour with boats clinking.
like a sky, placed light and orange clouds.
the clubs and their liquid shout clinking.
your tiredness, your reward at the small of your back.

your reward the hand at the back of the thigh,
the edge of the skirt, & firm.
a rest. firm as the body of a car, a body of
decisions made by others for you to rest on.
door cell stamped from steel coil. wet
window against the back of your back
or. the hard turn. resting in pressure.

let him watch, let him walk out to you
and watch. one close
as a hand as another watching
for your voice in
the symmetry of boats

Westwood Dusk

At the corner of Wiltshire and Westwood
what looked like a corpse
had collapsed on the sidewalk,
a smear of saliva
expressed from his lips.

Somebody glanced back,
sun setting on the sea
beyond wild thin frontage,
boulevards, palm trees
and a stoplight's countdown.

I stepped off and ran for my life.
That corpse was out cold
but breathing, and nobody
in the least fazed
at him gone west or westward . . .

With siren still sounding
a paramedic fire truck
drew up at the bus stop,
those people left standing
around as he lay.

Fixed under a sky glow,
Stranger Than Fiction
had opened at the Westwood Crest;
I was checking my direction
with best foot forward,
seeing and believing it there in LA.

Owning the Problem

'and it is but grief to have come home
if one cannot return to oneself.'
F. H. Bradley

Lath-ceilings down, through cracks
in the landing floorboards
and hall's revealed rafters,
there come light-chinks from below;
it's like that filmic nightmare
in which I tread, precarious,
on a tenement stair.

The broken light-chinks underline
a powder of blown plaster dust—
we're covered in it, see
how even soiled laundry
migrates from room to room
in this unfixed home
or stays put, as it must.

*

They put me in mind of emergency floor
lighting, or lights at the end
of a tunnel with stripped bedroom door
forming an exit before me.

Down the fracture lines, light-chinks lead
back where we'll begin again;
and I feel my way over joists through pitch darkness
as if above the Siberian plain . . .

*

So much that had to be postponed
returns with the light-chinks in your eye

it's like, despite a severe headwind,
past promises were renewed as we try,
heaven knows, to strike the note
of home (or get tradesmen to quote).

Enigmas of Departure

for John Matthias

It was while I walked out to the plane
readied on an apron at Giuseppe Verdi airport,
hair raised by the breeze
and a few spots of rain
spattering the tarmac,
across its spaces came a sense
of release in roaring silence
before being cabined, cribbed, confined . . .
And while I walked out from the gate
it caught me once again
as at South Bend, Michiana,
since we also had to wait
while our O'Hare plane arrived,
and the Michiana field
hazes off equally in a great plain . . .
Not that much wanting to go or to stay
but exposed in their flatness,
what I would fleetingly feel
from another winter's journey in the vastness
was an isolate air around frame houses
in yards out beyond wide sidewalks and a green
expanse, right, then a grey one
as we were cleared for take-off and were gone
to put yet more distance between.

Mortgaged Time

At the calm point of our summer,
I let a soul in torment
fly out through kitchen windows.
One abandoned villa front
had row on row of shutters
dangling by their hinges.
We'd found ourselves among the ruins
of a family's histories.
Sore eyes
took in the cool, quick-flowing waters.

Where a demolition process
was helped by rampant ivy,
tangles of intestines
hung from warehouse roofs;

through their shard-edged windows,
a start of pigeon wings
took flight for open air.
They at least had made their moves.

Everybody knows
we're working off the mortgaged time,
snatching at securities
as it runs fast through cupped fingers.
Paying back the past, a loan
we took out on ourselves,
you hold fast till a touch of breeze
revivifies the evening leaves—
living in hope, love, as the saying goes.

Broken Tiles

Hans Prinzhorn was a German psychiatrist and art historian whose *Artistry of the Mentally Ill* (1922) explored the relationship between mental illness and artistic expression and is considered a landmark in the history of outsider art.

Prinzhorn died in 1933 in Munich, having retired there with an elderly relative after the failure of his marriages. The building he had lived in was stripped for renovation as a chiropractic clinic in 1986; in the cellar a number of his patients' works were discovered, including a large crate of hand-painted ceramic tiles. Most were smashed, but a significant remnant were able to be pieced together with some hope of accuracy; a selection of these reconfigured tiles is presented below.

F O L K

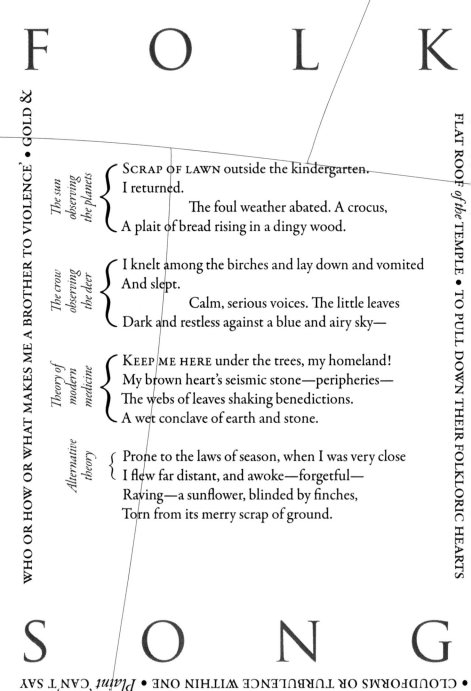

The sun observing the planets

{ SCRAP OF LAWN outside the kindergarten.
I returned.
   The foul weather abated. A crocus,
A plait of bread rising in a dingy wood.

The crow observing the deer

{ I knelt among the birches and lay down and vomited
And slept.
   Calm, serious voices. The little leaves
Dark and restless against a blue and airy sky—

Theory of modern medicine

{ KEEP ME HERE under the trees, my homeland!
My brown heart's seismic stone—peripheries—
The webs of leaves shaking benedictions.
A wet conclave of earth and stone.

Alternative theory

{ Prone to the laws of season, when I was very close
I flew far distant, and awoke—forgetful—
Raving—a sunflower, blinded by finches,
Torn from its merry scrap of ground.

S O N G

MARSH

Physiology of the genus

> BLACK-FIGURED. Chitinous of thought,
> Love-fearing. So I am. And from each wound
> I bear, exude a hæmolymphous spit,
> Simple and inhuman. But my *friend*

Indignity & iniquity

> Soothes me, his staff bathe my wings.
> Five times have their sticks mishandled me,
> Ugly and earthbound, firing the smoky BANGS
> Loudly that brought me down from the refectory.

A sacred promise

> NO, MY ORDER, I shall not abandon you.
> Evening's the time I shall alter and fly from this land.
> So shall the keeper accede and be altered to know
> Secrets of ours, who now is the rope on my neck, and

Reiteration of current folly

> Explicates at length the madness of a face
> Some god has painted on my carapace.

MOOD

R O U N D E L

Logistical necessities: materials, land, the love of others

WHITEWASH FOR MARKINGS, graphite and foolscap,
Rotas for observation of the skies,
Infinities, metalwork, carts of canvas,
Goodwill of your attendants. Survivals of hope,
HONESTY, Professor, your soul's fly's loop-the-loop
Towards the chasms of daring I suggest.

BARBITURATES, perhaps. And apple schnapps,
Rowdiness of the beer-hall, the great yeast
Of our short incarnations as the Living.
Together, you and I, I and my shadow,
How shall the dogs bark, how shall the winds blow
East over the wide field I need for landing,
Red sun in our eyes,
          we, should you cede what my mind is worth,
Shall stride in miles across
          the mangels the heads of those who stay on earth.

P I T / I R I S

D A M A S K

Binoculars slavering

WHAT BYZANTINE PRINCESS stepped across
The threshold of the censer's smoke — or priestess
Wept — as in her eye the sickly blue
Survives the lashes, a bird's egg dropped into
A nest of twigs blackened by the rain,
Pomp and plumage of the rarely seen —

WHETHER the insect-eating flower will bloom
To make my gorging rage a bed and tomb —

An arch of light

Or show sombre speechlessness of limb,
Inert, angelic breasts, her eye a boy's
Jewel of disdain; her girlhood slide away
Inside a charcoal frame and hieratic air and rain —

These chipped ceramic pearls — a single tentacle uncurls —

H E A R T B U R N

POLY-

2 *Problem*

{

DOPPELGÄNGER falling in the dark,
Blood-loosened from time's unity.
Strange sunset colour of the sow's
Decomposing stench. A forceful twin's
Emergence, sheen-deep proof-of-evil,
Sectional towering, kaleidoscope gathering
Fool's gold, the swine-fleeing angel.

•

1 *Solution*

{

CORPUS CONCLAVE of miniscules. Host
Fearful and lowly. Lucid river at sunrise,
Flowering, ascension from a primal chamber,
Sight-wrangler, to and from elsewhere,
Vengeful glider, limbs of the twin of the wind.
Maniacal sunrise of LOVE'S dimensions, forlorn,
Co-sensing, heart fluttering of the bird.

PHYSITE

FAIRY

Bloom rises

Two EMPERORS AND A POPE slump on a bench,
A bunch of hunching tramps, a rats' nest,
Or statesmen sleeping off a splendid lunch

The flowering

Thus to dream of the *unloveliest*
Predicament: to lurk friendless and alone,
Silent in winter's ilex heart, to leach
In a dark corner of a sodden park,
While gurgling glossolalic churns, the urns,
Their STOMACHS, turn the last meal to ash—

The dawn

When wordless, patterned colour comes: a *spark*
Hovers above the dead three lying there—

They are sleeping

Star, tsaritsa, wrist of light, a spire
Twisting in the blazing blue-green host,
The claimant forest wind, the angels' ghosts.

TALE

Lynne Hjelmgaard

Who brought you to this place?

Disappear into the park
early, after a sleepless night

in the toilet the smiling Signora, Gracia

is black, white and red tiramisu
is cypress trees at the top of the stairs

a man sings his a's, e's and o's
everyone needs Borghese

the poets the ballerina the man reading his paper
the actors the parakeets the painter
who paints the scene of this poem

as magnolia
as conversation
as a grieving angel writes
on Lord Byron's face

'there is that within me which shall'

as young as old
as already gone

after forty nine days the soul
leaves the first place of light

cicadas take the lead
followed by swallows tweet-ing
geese cackling

the baby bird turns to dust
David fights the lion
Hadrian builds Antinopolis
for the boy who fell into the Nile

the first year it throbs
then numbs out
to less, moves
up through the throat
shortens the breath

to move in waves the way
the world does
when someone says your name

Title: from Brenda Hillman's untitled fragments, Bright Existence.

Villa Borghese

this is the afternoon of running water
the scent of urine, coral beneath an archway
covered in soot

a man lame and blind begs in the hot sun, Yes
this is his afternoon
of cicadas, a popping cork

tourists wading in fountains
his sudden cry, wailing arms, steaming
hill, heat

a fall flat on my face
thou art in the garden of the world
dirt in my mouth

his torn pants his no teeth his one finger raised
we are headless statues
scattered white feathers in mud

a water jet glistens
out of a mask
to the brim of marble bubbling

Where a rose has left you wounded

spring brings me deep
into the blossoming forest
where your tulips grow

a hawk chases a gull or swallow
shrieks, cries of other birds
behind the shadow
of a Roman hedge

a tiny belly pants with breath
its twisted beak and flat wings
crushed on the dusty ground

the night isn't finished
I guide you back to bed

*

the easiest path
to the sea
is through the wild roses
the peeling lounge chairs
on the terrace, lavender
where the deer sleeps
in the morning

headless tulips
a smell of soap
on the body
wood
carry wood

afterwards, no longer him
alive there——

Title: from Jerome Rothenberg's The Lorca Variations *(XXI, 'The Return')*
Final couplet from Mallarmé's A Tomb for Anatole, *33.*

A number of interpretations of this dream are available

After wandering around for some hours I
returned to the landing place but before
reaching it was overtaken by a tropical storm.
Why should this story have become fixed
In my mind until it became an agonising
obsession? To effect an entrance was not so
easy but would any self-respecting pirate
give up an opportunity to talk about her youth.
Something in the form of the girl irresistibly
recalled his dream of the figure in the bath
yet the afternoon was hot & an intolerable
oppression reigned. The boards creaked
a good deal as I moved around & the signs
of occupation were so recent that I could
hardly believe I was alone. There, among the
correspondence, was a letter from the pirate.

Last night Alice had a curious dream, yet it's
good to know that knobbly fruit & vegetables
are back on the menu. Meanwhile, outside
the smokehouse, something fishy is going on.
Flamboyant millionaires & retired buccaneers
have bought up much of the land, displacing
small-time dealers with coffee shops & boutiques.
In civilian hands the tattoo is used to assert
individuality although not everyone is joining
the queue for the summer of love. At last, the
pirates conspired together & hit upon a plan
that promised a dazzling victory. They were
off the leash & on the lash. In the long run,
lending across frontiers can only be serviced
by trading surpluses, yet we now recycle a
third of all our rubbish.

Some sailors suffer loneliness in a crowd
while others become lonely when there is
not a soul in sight. A death wish or something
like it may be present in all of us yet the rise
& fall of hemlines is reckoned to correspond
with the ups & downs of the economy. As he
hurried from the library, I was conscious of
the circle of bewilderment he had left behind.
A terrible desire came upon me to rid the
world of such a monster. Refreshments will
include a free wine-tasting & a hog roast
in the stable courtyard yet we have little to
do but meet & greet. Most dandies have a
Peter Pan complex yet a great advantage of
working with dead people is that their
objections go unheard.

Let's consider other people's words & how we misuse them

Many are the actors & pirates who
rely on others putting words into their
mouths. Here already is the rich
aromatic breath of resins, a presage
of the smell of pinewoods & summer
days. Yet how could such a tiny,
wingless creature reach the empty
island so quickly? Perhaps the difference
is merely a matter of tone yet pirates
are crippling themselves with impact
exercises. Although salt is very much
derided these days, we still have a
deep desire & craving for something
fishy. Interest is fixed for twelve months,
calculated daily on the cleared balance
& paid at maturity.

One thing is certain: offering steady employment with benefits & holiday pay is a practice which has fallen out of economic fashion. With hits like *Don't you want me, baby*, The Human League took an art agenda onto the high street. There were bottles flying everywhere but the pirates simply decided to carry on with their performance. Waterspouts pick up fish & transport them live to nearby lakes & streams. It's a good thing we don't have to apply these rules to potential lovers. There is some evidence that this process is underway yet today you can sail close by the islands without ever guessing their violent history.

Fish, to the Mesopotamians, were majestic creatures, yet it's time to step off the scale & get out the tape measure. What has prompted France's youth to turn from sensible tipplers into full-time abusers? For their part, the factory owners are in no rush to expand the size of their workforce, so you really get the flavours dancing in your mouth. Pirates don't come to enjoy the floats & the music, they come to commit acts of violence. Let's consider other peoples' words & how we misuse them. More to the point, aren't our campuses supposed to be overflowing with troublemaking, tenured radicals? Yet every sea has its own characteristic which contributes to the texture of pirate society.

Michael Ayres

Love poems like autopsies

In bright light your bodies sway and lie
in love poems like autopsies.
There are the capuccinos and the old cord jacket
of washed-out lime
and biscuit chinos, white T.
This is too true to be good you say
as Alfie steers his pale blue car into traffic,
puts on some music and laughs.

She gets off the bed and pads away across the room.
Through the Venetian blinds the moon is rising.
You pour out the city from the secret place
in which you keep the things
which are not immediate,
shake out the streets,
the innumerable little wells of loneliness,
dustbins, service ducts, steel shutters,
but it is somebody else's loneliness today,
so you let your gaze rise with the moon
in unearthly sympathy.
From the rooves of skyscrapers, steam from the air-con units
drifts in plumes
like the ghosts of bombs.
She comes back and slips off her robe,
and you stop rolling the dice of your thoughts
and kiss her.
Somewhere, the dice still tumble
into valleys of carbon and moss
and your kisses have become
small beads of fresh rainwater
falling on stones.
A silence opens inside you
and she fills you with her breathing.
She has touched the sea and now she touches you.
The sea moves with her fingers.

When she leaves she takes the sea with her
and you will never hear the sound of waves again.
But you hear them now . . .

You will be with her soon. From the window seat
as the plane banks sharply
the city slides and glides
in a casual astronomy
of fluid stars.
The trickling corpuscles of traffic,
synapses sparkling on cocaine,
melt into the odour of her skin
as she steps from the ocean.
You have loaded her with such absurd expectations,
yet the strange thing is that, for a while,
she carries them.
She has become hope, your diary teems with her,
she is every direction you move in.
The engines rev and then go quiet
and the jet seems to float upwards towards the moon again,
away from earth.
You lie back and rest your head in her long black hair,
it pours and coils down on your face
and far from the bodhi tree
just this small cluster of delicate sensations
makes you happy.

There are days when she brushes against you
with her hip or the edge of her hand
it sends a shock of peace through you.
The tiniest contacts
make you dizzy
as if you were high on some precipice
and you can't quite tell whether falling
will mean rapture, or calamity,
or both.
Then you fall,
then she no longer touches you.
In between there is knowledge,

but it is just the air moving
between the wings of a flying bird.

It was not in the snow, or it was only in the snow
to an infinitesimal degree, as the corpse
is in the shadow.
Or perhaps it swept through the snow
entirely, permeated the fairy lattice of each flake
as substantially
as a memory permeates a mind.
Swept through the white forest like a fire.
Like hands through hair.
Caribou crop at the low branches.
In the hinterland of other people's lives,
the immense systemic calm of a world without focus,
destiny flattens out and the stars are too many
to count or to care for.
In serialised homes, the hum of unseen commuter trains
threads an anonymous life of things,
and to the wallow and whine of washing machines,
lost in local daydreams
individual figures take on
the thoughtless peace of appliances.
In the soft wheels run and run,
penned softly within conducive routines.
Subaudible, humdrum robots beep and click, like insects meeting.
Underfoot, the arena of skyscrapers and daytime TV
crushed among the giant ants.
And glaciers weep no tears.
With the mute compliance of barometers,
these devices perform their tasks again and again;
as the lovers bliss up to the music and sigh,
the production line of DNA
runs off another model like Chinese toys.
Like Aztec ruins, on suburban lawns,
white plastic furniture lies tipped over
abandoned to the sudden rain.

Ghost of a pearl

You hold her it is a moment of brilliance
and a little later you enter
the sensual nirvana of orgasm
It's like a cloth you let fall slowly permitting its redness
to slip through your hands like a rope of water
You do not thrust it away
but neither do you seek to restrain it
Then somehow it has gone
to the place where all unthought-of things drift
and gather
There it begins its long wait
calmly, as in truth it must
The way her hair stirred towards the corner of her mouth
in the draught from the window
The fragile shadow of the naked bulb on the ceiling
hung like the ghost of a pearl
The sweatbeads each with their own tiny portion of light
flesh stars and salt until you cool right off
a breathing lustre . . .

The restless moment waits for you
In the cafeteria with the blue plastic trays on the steel rails
In the railway station where the air
is punctuated by the disembodied voices of tannoys
In your children's arms and your children's eyes
the restless moment waits for you
waits for you with the years

You check your watch
She is late
It is almost reassuring
The mysterious weight of the banal collects itself around you
and you impart to it that haunting spin
which is special to you
Books displayed in Border's window
stacked in little pyramids

Shoppers and the reflections of shoppers
A lyre's glisten of spokes and the black seal lycra
of the racing cyclists strolling past
The sky above the buildings the clouds sluggish with incipient rain
The things you will say to her
The way you will wait for the first moment
she will stroke back her hair
and take up a strand
and twist it round her fingers
so that some small and obscure rightness will happen
a settlement in the world
allowing things to proceed
despite the international chaos and the worsening domestic situation
and the death of the goldminers
and fears about the price of gold

The cranes over the void where the old buildings used to stand
and the new buildings will rise
The equine flicker of the dials as you start the car
and rev the engine
The new music you have brought
to replace the music which has turned to silence
The silence which floods in like a tide
filling the rock pools of failed conversations
with glitter and salt
Tears your love becomes and then
that silence again, somehow benign, peaceful,
utterly replete
The sea with its waves, the spume rolling
like a fleece endlessly shorn
And beneath the water, the involved
and patient industry of oysters,
barnacles and clams—
mute, secreting things
The call of the voiceless moon in spring
The way you wake beside each other and you give youselves again
to the fleeting erasure of dawn

Dead Men's Shoes

On the Pest bank of the Danube, near Parliament House, there are iron shoes in pairs . . . their owners, who never wore them in their lives, were shot from the bank in the autumn and winter of 1944–45 for the capital crime of being Jewish. The patriots of the Arrow Cross committed this deed, under the Árpád flag now rehabilitated at political demonstrations—then, and now in some hands, it was a symbol of a Turanian wonderland unsullied by Semites, Roma, and interlopers from the mongrel Atlantic. They did so as, on the Buda bank, the turul-bird of Magyar legend perched proudly on the Castle Hill walls . . . and either exalted in their ruthlessness or, with a certain degree of resignation, performed a solemn yet, in their minds, unavoidable act of national hygiene.

Sixty years later, they are despised by all apart from the most intransigent of fascists, and Budapest—no less a Jewish city than a Hungarian one—is, above all else, a city that belongs to the world. But these iron shoes, scattered on the bank in a quiet place without traffic, where cheap leather shoes were taken off before the shots rang out from behind, speak of utter homelessness. They are worn by ghost-people with invisible yellow stars who act, as witnesses, to suffering and ignominious death. They express the vulnerability of human beings in the face of armed barbarity, but also the possibility—the possibility only—of eventual vindication and memorial.

They are not shoes of a kind I am ever likely to wear, although this has often been said. They are not shoes of a kind my friends are ever likely to wear, although this has been said, as often, and with less conviction.

Chastened by seeing them, unexpectedly, on an iron-blue day beside the Danube I continue north—tempted, despite my exhaustion, to cross the next bridge. It's as if I were expecting to see wet footprints on the opposite bank.

Bells Drowned in Air

for Béla Tarr

I chased the doctor through stubble fields, as mud squelched over my boots. He had been prised from his pickling-jars of apricot brandy, decanted one litre at a time, by the sound of bells from the disused church—not heard from that direction in years. All alone in that desolate hamlet, he had put down his notebook and waddled, bearing his body-fat on guy-ropes of blood, too heavy and too indomitable to die. I cased him from a distance, conscious of crows.

The bell, just one of them in fact, was low-toned—it clanged as rain-clouds massed. I followed the doctor, the director and the crew. I was in three places at once—my own, the director's, and the sad grey landscape I had scanned, at high speed, from Intercity trains on their way to Nyíregyháza or Békéscsaba. So it was that, mingled with the bell, I heard the jingle that was played to accompany station announcements, along with the rapid machine-gun fire of vowels and consonants from female announcers. But this faded and all I could hear, then, was the dreary tone of the bell.

The doctor reached the church, gasping for breath in over-used air like a washed-up whale. The sky, grown indolent in summer, had retained its rubbery thickness. It pressed him down and the bell, too, was strangely muffled—all the more so the closer he got. Pummelling space, it dived to the threshold of hearing.

In the bell-tower, perhaps ten metres above the ominous flatness of the puszta, a madman banged the bell with a stick. I stood beside the camera, watching the doctor as he watched the madman... but the madman took no notice, he kept on, saying over and over 'The Turks are coming! The Turks are coming!'. His eyes, that claimed the camera's focus, were as full moons eclipsed by solar shadow.

The doctor waddled back to his house where he boarded up the windows, decanted himself another litre of apricot brandy, then pickled his flesh against that horrible sound—to be found again in the spring, impossibly dead or alive. I took the madman's place and am banging that bell, in a space a hundred metres deep in the back of my head, as he strides out into the world each morning— as confident as a pasha, inspecting his captured lands.

What I Wanted To Say About György Ligeti

The dematerialisation's as immense as ever—geographies of sound diffuse into cirrus patterns seen from an aircraft at midday. Solaris illusions fool me into seeing what I loved and has passed forever, cities and clock-towers and trees that wave in parks and cyclists moving under them as pigeons and starlings scatter.

All of this is melting, steaming, forming and un-forming and the colours that reflect this mingling are unearthly, eerie, as delicate as those in a nebula, firework colours out of Stravinsky made still more ethereal and extreme . . . so tenuous in their evasion of mind and tongue, in a world of ceaseless and hyperactive change where clocks become clouds and clouds are sugar watches melting in sun, everything resisting the solidity that is death.

You wove all this, candyfloss flavoured with the dark blood of your sombre heritage, the pain of a clown's there if we look for it and you laid it down lightly, your lost Erdély, slow carts trundling between bare hills, ramshackle villages with long main streets, manic dances and yellow stars in the air.

In protean transformations from the grave to the sky, your music lent itself so perfectly to the acid overdrive of the spaceman's escape and its chromo-delirium. You spent your life in take-off, winging from difficult roots as, that autumn week in 1956, you escaped the institute, the imprisoned country and crossed a continent to sleep, for days, on arrival as if in pupation. You evaded the trap of what you would have been, a caterpillar in a tomb of thick glass, a professor growing old in a mellowing city, to deal firsthand and on equal terms with the Tao.

Your brain has become anonymous dust but we can listen and dream with your thoughts and, each birthday, sharing yours I can't help but try to resurrect you. Looking at clouds in a late spring sky, I can hear the infinite droplets of your music. And all notes remain possible—even the classical remains as everything warms, expands, grows strange and mobile in the quickening world.

Norbert Hummelt   *translated by Catherine Hales*

berlin fresco

stüler is quite expecting mould as he inspects the tower
of saint mary's. they can't ventilate the nave properly: there's
a lot of damp in these old walls and it's creeping upwards.
but the plaster just here has a strange sound. the royal chief architect

taps a bit of the chalky layer off. so now they who have gone
into the still wall now come to light little by little: faces leached
of colour whitewashed over each day's area done by the fresco painter
as he applied the paint to the still-moist plaster. which has to be done

quickly for the plague is at the door: another soul captured
in stone. but death takes each one by the hand: the thin man
in his white robe the picture the crumbling script that speaks
again and again of just one thing: mr monk i would just like to say

something: see how well i can dance before you all . . god every
time I hear that i'm so sorry i still want to get this and that
finished and make it to the rhine just one more time the way it looks
in the old engravings . . and then fade for ever into the wall

blues

the light broke through the glass blocks again and
played over the tiles, the parquet, showing how yawn-
ingly empty the room was, for there was not so much
as a bed in the house. nor did it echo as it did just so
recently, which was probably because no-one was
speaking; I went slowly through the empty rooms while
the light was breaking through glass blocks. we haven't
seen these glass blocks for a long time when there was
furniture here we didn't notice them it was a winter's day
and outside the sun was shining that didn't fit into my
scheme of things I went through the empty rooms again.

then on top of that the sound of birdsong came in from
outside which I was not quite able to ignore. the light
broke through the glass blocks again I could not fail to
see it so I thought it better to go back down to the base-
ment where there was still an old mirror hanging in the
hobby room. I could see eyes in it, but they were not only
mine. there were people dancing, they were behind me.
there were peanut flips on the lino. music was playing
and a record was jumping. I turned around, but saw no-
one dancing. no flips on the floor, only dust and silence
and light pushing weakly through the basement window.

memling's madonna

was completely unknown to me until I found the small
framed picture lying in the dust while I was clearing out
the cellar. a head-and-shoulders portrait, no lap, no holy

child, no angels to be seen either. you cannot see much
else apart from mary's face, eyes meditative, a small mouth,
brownish foliage as background; but I like the small

tender ear and am not averse to her light brown hair, the
dark red stola thrown over it, as worn by roman women
in the street and in the bazaar. but I have absolutely no

idea how this picture came to be in the cellar, who brought
it here and why; maybe it was no longer any use for praying
to, seemed to be dispensable with as protection in the

night, could no longer even be considered as decoration
on the wall above the sleeping child. but still the old art
shines, the cheap print stuck on a bit of wood.

constable

in some of john constable's pictures I can only
ever see clouds the way as though they could
move they hang motionless over the meadows

of salisbury. then the light falls then the mood
changes it's briefly banished beneath
the clouds: effects of light on the mood

are something I'm only too well aware of. I've been
looking at clouds half the day today the way they
were forming changing passing over white and with

threatening dark edges and was lying still as a landscape.
a few evenings ago it seemed to me as though
there was a blue cloud in the sky I called you and

wanted to show you you came outside and saw it
clearly: over the city a blanket of cloud through which
we could briefly see something else, something bright.

dance of death

fear of the dark is not the whole story. we hardly
know each other and don't really want much more,
the long hot summer is over and the only traffic jam
was near cologne but going in the other direction.
the barn is in the haze, the drizzle of the flat land.
It's not often that I'm the one who puts the music on.
we know each other so well and are becoming more
and more like strangers. the old score is all that stays
put in our minds. this is nothing for gentler spirits, the
racket, the posing, and the quantities of beer, but once
I found in all of this many tender wonders, and if they
came back I'd have no objection. fear of the dark leaks

from all the speakers, the lighting console can do no-
thing on its own; there's no disco ball, no dry ice. only
one song in five is still able to get our legs twitching,
but there's no more sparkle in our eyes .. if only the fog
were to come into the barn and enfold the dancing fig-
ures: in the haze, the drizzle of the flat land images are
flitting; but only the dance of the dead can be so wild.

crossing

the wind is working among the chestnut trees. I used to
walk along this avenue as a child: it's blocked off now
because of the danger of branches breaking off. it led
from the monastery to schloss dyck via the dyck wine
house in damm the way led back to the monastery. inside
is dark and cool as always. I dip my hand into the font
cross myself in the nave I see the brass plates in the floor
with the names of the von salm-reifferscheidt family. in the
wall an epitaph (marble). the person resting here was once
a count: the first death's head I saw in my life. the bones
jutting out from the relief like the vein in father's temple
when he was laid low with one of his headaches I was
asked to massage him the vein pulsing my fingers stroking
his hot brow, along the cold stone. two tablet halves daily
he always took me with him on his walks to the water but
there was no barque, no ferryman, no styx in the monastery
garden the jüchener stream marked the boundary between
cologne and aachen. we'd be across it in a single step.

Hendrik Jackson   *translated by Catherine Hales*

from weather fields

DRAWING WATER

I

depressing these squalls forecast a while ago, pressing
into our backs—a stone thudded dully on to the asphalt, at some point
I spoke (*tipsily*) about understatement. a bonn karneval procession passed
along the spree. I ran again across the same square, which seemed empty

—a change of weather favoured decisions. erosion of colour
warm and cold air layers, fragments of images in eyelashes
then driving rain masses spraying a metre high, atomising on roof ridges
as you were easing off, a little sun broke through the veil— (*still*)

II

in the antechamber at twelve o'clock at night (*a heavy feeling*)
now and again the great door opened—outside
the air was smouldering with electricity
the thunder rolling right across the sky

the break-up of the layers and bright as blinking
the asphalt lit up as though from inside
(*dead light*) and the shaking of a ball of fabric
in the grip of a gigantic dog

III

—passing through: past wooden slats slagheaps wooden bars, disused
land (*behind the dream*) in the enclosed district, somewhere
mediterranean breezes arose, your amazement, the body: a casing—
dark, the air let in. in the streets, when you turned up:

your (*only in the moment*) body photographed to exhaustion, liquid amber
on roofs, stones, now you all disappeared behind the windwalls
someone counted the half dark in, it wavered. spotlight, echo
of a clicking, closed aperture, more images pouring in

CHARGES

I

your face in the light. warm concrete pillars corner
a spanish girl coming near, a (*swollen*) handbag
you hold the edge a moment, you see:
in the dark a (*curved*) swan's neck, traced through

—a few images later—on to desire. it gives
pleasure (*the reef, in the silence: foaming*) the shiver
of fear. like a drink cool in the crowd (*legs*)
short gasp. changing brightness of strips on your neck

II

crass—the way everything interlinks: branch and sky's capillary
a hurricane rolling up—strong—the gravel clawing chewing and tow
collapsing softly. (*silvery: sounds*) trumpeting, shooting up
into the weeds beaten down, where treacherous fragments

between flaring up and forgiving—are extinguished. vibrates under
warm hand: charged particles, ground loosened
at the wall the jagged tear goes—almost to the roots—
auspice of pensive latecomers, senselessly leaned against

III

the numbers remain a secret. the queues for the government offices
and the stiffened faces gave rise to guesses
something flashed in his back (*clair*). a joke surely
—nothing precise recognisable, dawn a rump

swept away the buildings. swept away the flickering
particles. data carriers, which due to the weather registered
nothing. light failure (*liaisons*). what remained seemed
unimportant, made a sudden rush of white noise, dived—dark currents

ANGLES OF INCIDENCE

I

we cleared out warehouses, made a chain
to pass the pistons—pretty hot out there, pressure
on our hands and the possibility seemed easy
of unexpected death . . . the brief summer of '37

on the lookout (*reloading*) sun-soaked
courtyard, kastanienallee. next to the fodder sheds
watching a (*precise*) fall of light on the faggot
of wood the wall the detail of the storm before evening

II

a small star in the corner of your eye, like flakes someone softly
dozing there, friend, a heavy rolling started, fracto
cumulus *covered signs the sky formations, changeable—*
approaching frost and the sun on the other side . . . thus memories

distanced themselves, burdened beneath growing heaps, drifts
—rippling. words, alike as two peas, snowed over on the inside (*blooming*)
leaden, laborious climbing—slumber with no holds, distant blue
cleft (*sheer*) snow shimmer blackness, glimmers dark air

III

so as that region in its entirety is unknown to us, its inhabitants are still
completely unknown too . . . *we can only assume that there are more*
sunny inhabitants in the sun region . . . on that day the air
was heavy and approximate coming days made us happy unfulfilled

good memory, weather: frictions dischargings, that shows
that no equation, especially with strangers, could ever be solved
—drift of light, earth shadows. you fell with sleep into one. like
lead (*sluice train*) silvery—creel bream dreamed it, floodings

SKETCHES OF TRANSIENCE

I

was that clouds? see the frost-white (*shaken*) valleys
the magnificence of golden mountings, frothing
white (*symmetrically*) fluffy with sharply-focused edges on one side. full
        stop
two dashes: movements of gulls, napkins of the soul (*auguries*)

—familiar warmth, plus-minus connotations. *you could lean
into the yorkshire wind like into a living hedge*
then: *deep trembling, transparent blue.* there, you see. closeness of the air,
swarms distant from earth, childhood bobbles, wide-skied yearning

II

shuddering, remembering (*weather-illuminated*) weeks, reckless
starch streaks in the sky, a misty veil all along the horizon driving waves
before it. considerations, lasting after-darkening of heavy material (*globe*)
landscape crouching after rain. sensitivity to weather changes, more
        than the sum

of the molecules——full moon and tiny needles, constable still working
on his final study (*see turner cited by ruskin*) platanenallee now
golden-orange (*planet*)—well diced for, we didn't want more than that
        (*glory*)
on the steps of the palace—motionless. dice, random, left lying

III

at last glorious weather fields, the clouds gone. the end
its own precondition (*never thought of that?*)—i dodged—hit—
sideways . . . after all, i don't talk in opposites, but wait
now and again (*blinded*) for a good word, on the crumbling side

of the wall, previously: brief confusion, when we unexpectedly
met, it imprinted itself on my memory how her hair fell into her face,
then,
full of thoughts (*no, just with a skinful*) wobbling into a clearing
falling asleep with familiar weather conditions, head sunk to my chest—

Fruit

The mother lies dead before her mother and the hybrid riverbed awaits for new rain in the mould of wasted soil.

And the tree drives shrapnel on children, the hosts slide through white wine.
And on the bloodied rick night lingers, the grass ruminates a sun on the prairie.

The children graze the empty well that almost floods the meadow, searching for their father in circles and horns.

The bull child pours forth a scream and is born!

Before the eternal path of twilight, the earliest fruit of a virginal race seasons the entire tree facing the river.

Third Letter to the Father

Sewing your name on the empty tree is sewing your sweet absence on your nonbeing. Now it is all light and sugary pool, easy conscience of the wettest tar. No one swept the brow in my memory; sticks sprouted: forthcoming fruit.

The sun fashions a father in me and you will be the father no more. I'll be the fruit taken from your tree with my own hands: blood of your blood.

May the bull cry horns from his eyes; may he rush into the olive woman's sex,—so the children may matter no longer; so the children may remain children!

Second Sexual Identity

Today no one searches for the armless edge where the sheath drinks the wine and overbrims, opposing margins walk today to the drift of that

blackest flower.
Humid gods over the pillow's open rump crown me flesh with the sweat of manacled milk.

I was born high like the goddess and high shall die like the white mother on the dreamed breasts of what's concave.
And the swans anoint necks beneath the anus
and I dream a tragic origin of dung.
And the honeyed orchards strip,

—no children are born in between stone brows!

Man's Animal Monologue

The moribund mother braids summer on her inert crown, and ages fountain-full of dry honey and clay, full of river and rose on her dawn. She denies blood to the child she gave birth to, so that he may give birth to his blood and betroth a new mother.

Mother and wife kiss their beloved, their offering falls amid flesh and is born. The jar of light is split and the child is left alone, unbound. Roses float on the blood river, rise slowly over the white mountain, want to anoint their petals on the sky.

Sewing the Snow or The Mother's Death

The bull brought his offering on his head, dressed the wild flower in humid horns; his honey traced the freshest roses, milk sweetness in which to open the dung-psyche. The snow sewed fringes on the bodice, the son kissed the Father, and the light cord touched the mother-soft silence. If the woman unties the tragic string of veins by the tree of life, heaven and earth would thread in the garden, and the son would grow healthy, horned and holy. So that a sweeter flower may drift along this riverbed of new and cold water, the mother lies dead by the river.

Barefoot

The writing's upper part can't be read,
Nor is it clear who wrote it.
Anyway, it's the words, not the sound, that counts.

". . . Then I ate whatever I found in the house:
bread, almonds, cress.
I jumped barefoot onto the horse,
So wild was the morning's wine,
And off I went through the people
At full gallop."

Forgive Us All

They were sitting, drinking in the rain
with their hair ruffled like soil
a crate of lager, vodka too . . .
The women looked pale, thin, unhappy.
But October wasn't yet over.

I recognized her the second I saw her.
"Hello" I said, "don't you recognize me?
We pulled your corpse from the sea
fully clothed.
And yes, you swaggered as you walked . . ."

"I'd forgotten", she said, "forgive me."

In the Sun

Because the hours are few, they don't catch it all,
They're undone in the sun and slip away.
As the corn grows strong the gardener
Quietly worries about the drought.
Silent birds, a goat, heavy olive trees.
A car passed on the narrow road
Somebody waved, perhaps someone we knew,
Perhaps not, a sign of transience.
And in the weary age of the sea, ivy
On the balcony quivers with children's screams,
Because they're few, the hours, a second can't hold
The sea, daydreaming, and the geranium.
Wind whipped up and carried the fisherman's boats
To far-off swordfish, we will never know
In what depth they fertilize the sea
As they steer on gravely to the east.

And just now the smell of soup on the stove
Finds the nose of the dog and cat.
Books on the shelf, a blue bottle and a rose
Were separately frozen apart.
A picture on the wall of a crowded
Village green, children, a hoop and time;
How Breughel brought them together
In one harmonious whole
Because the hours are few, there is no room,
And all is undone in the sun and slips away.

Dream

I saw a dream while I was napping
Light snow was falling
Sabahat sat up in her sick-bed
And was looking at a light
Light snow was falling
My mother was weeping in Erzincan
Thinking of my brother the sailor.

It was snowing.

Tulip

I undressed you with my hands,
Like spring opening petals,
Your impatience seeded like a pomegranate.

Oh songs of the breathing forest,
The heart of kisses and looks,
Questions in its thronging silence.

Your desire's roof soared in the sky,
Humming yellow butterflies
Burst out on all sides.

I tied you down with my teeth
Like an insatiable silkworm,
Your redness cleft like the moon

Two slices of tulip on the sheets.

Özdemir Asaf   *translated from Turkish by George Messo*

Dialogue

One day, in a house, there was
a cat.
That day, in a house, that cat
Didn't begrudged me its warmth.

That day, in that house, that cat
took me away, brought me back.
I sang my songs to him;
he slept, I looked on, he was with me.

An unexpected event occurred;
he teased the coils of former days.
Was it there, it wasn't, as if there
the cat was on my lap.

My eyes were in its eyes,
its eyes were in mine too.
Its paws scratched my hands...
I shuddered, suddenly trembled inside.

One day, in a house, there was
a cat.
That day, in a house, that cat
took me from my distant childhood.

That day, in that house, that cat,
as if to say, look what's happened here,
brought me and left me in my youth.
In the gardens of memory a heat chilled.

It was June for months when my father died.
He was fifty-four, I was seven.
When a light went out the road lit-up.
How did the cat know these things.

There was a day, a house, and that cat
threw a stone down my well.
When it stopped in my spiny well
he sang lullabies.

This was like a story;
did I explain, did he listen.
Should I have kept quiet, or spoken;
neither it, nor that day, nor the cat were there.

The Story of the Cat Playing with the Candle Flame

I

A candle was burning in the room of a house.
There was a cat in the house too.
As nights went by of their own accord
The candle burned and the cat played.

On one such night when the candle burned
The cat became lost in its game.
In eyes hungry for play
The candle flame burned,
The cat stared,
And in the flickering flame of the candle
A toying pleasure called out.

The cat, growing in its games, grew too
In its own child-like way,
Went round and round, walked slowly
Towards the toy-like flame.
A glance, once more, and again it looked
And stretched a paw
To the flickering candle flame.
He appeared confused
Until his whiskers burned . . .

Didn't seem to believe
That the flame he'd seen for the very first time
Could burn him.

The cat grew as it played,
The candle grew cold as it burned.
Time stepped between them,
Quickened its pace.
And something seemed strange
Between the burning of one
And the games of the other.

But the cat grew as it played,
Slowly losing the game.
And the candle grew small as it burned,
Slowly losing its flame.

The cat, as it plays, will burn,
The candle, lighting, growing small, will burn.
The one getting small will brighten as it burns,
The one growing big will learn as it's burnt.

After the candle's burning
And the cat's playing
There remained
In a room of a house
In the middle of the night
Two people
Silently staring.

II

The candle burned to its end,
The cat grew and went.
Games dissolved into nights
Into a silent insomnia.

In the memories and thoughts
Of two people
A cat and a candle
Came and went.

Wherever a candle burns now,
Wherever a cat plays,
The shadows of each are entwined and reflect . . .
Today is like yesterday,
Yesterday like today.
The candle scratches my hands
And the cat's paws light up my past.

Edoardo Sanguineti　　　*translated from Italian by Ian Seed*

from Reisebilder (1971)

29

I wouldn't know how to write it anymore, for you, an infinite letter,
　　　on school paper
with regular lines, with decorations in red and blue pencil, with chains
of hearts and flowers, full of capital D (for Du, for Dein), of
für uns underlined forcefully:
　　　　　　　　　　　　(a letter like the one we spied
the other day, in the hands of two boyish civilians, on the top deck
of a 94 Bus):
　　　　　　　not even if you were that tiny pseudo-
hawaiian berliner girl without a breast, without a bra, who exhibited
　　　herself recklessly
for us: (for us, sitting to suck a banana ice cream, under
a small flag with the writing 'EIS', from a gallant ice-cream man who
　　　looks like
a butcher):
　　　　　　　not even if I was that obscene faun of middle
age which really I am, by this time:
　　　　　　　　　　　　look me in the face, at least
when you cut my hair on the balcony, because I'm there with naked
　　　torso, in the living
sun of midday, in the wind:
　　　　　　　　　　I dream of myself being similar to Hoffmann
in delirium: and I'm almost the double of a mediocre english comic:

from Purgatory of Hell (1960–1963)

11

oh (he said): if you write a poem for me; oh (he said): if you write,
you have to put that I waited for you at Gap, that I was crying, crying a lot;
if you really write for me (he said): oh you have to put that my brother
Alessandro was crying too, that he waited for you, and cried a lot: and
        that I slept,
that night, in a hotel;
        you have to write (he said): oh you have to write that at Pompei
they all died;
        that the fascists are wicked;
that the numbers never end . . .

14

and they were speaking, in the dark (and I, in bed, reading a novel by
        Sollers); and they were speaking
in the corridor, and were saying, perhaps (that is, something like): but
        he will, that one,
be all happy (because we enter like that, by surprise, in the night, his room,
in the dark); and they were speaking:
                then Anna was in the armchair; and
        Françoise (the second),
and Odile (and Edith), on my bed; and Anna was in pyjamas; and he woke
(in his bed); (and said: what do they want?);
                then they brought a blackboard,
with the idiocies of names deformed (and they were reading, all together,
out loud);
        then I said to Ollier
that he looked, he did, like one of the two priests of *Chien andalou*; and he
made a sad face (and said, then: am I so démodé, then?); (and
the *Chien andalou* is from '29, it seems; (and Thibaudeau
was shouting: but it's all like a novel; that is, mine); (and Roche was
        saying but we need
to switch off the light, here);

                      and I switched off the light, and switched it
         on, then switched it off
again; and I was saying, in the dark, but motionless:
                              but nothing is happening.

15

beyond that purgatory of gardens (and the white light, and the chairs
of iron); and (still) beyond the birds dying
in the green:
             there's the Galerie Vivienne;
beyond us, thus, that true cemetery exists (as I said): three long
boxes of picture postcards, all with writing, with stamps:
                              all of them to read.

16

just as they were saying: but look; (that moon; but right then
I was thinking (but calmly) of the words I wrote to my wife: 'but
calmly'; (having explained): 'but calmly' (later) 'for
ever' (that ominous meaning):
                   my feet
in wet grass, on the path, after the rain, uncertain, in the middle of norman
cows (.:.); and then the dawn, just so; and then Madame Heurgon, who
        saw us
from the castle window (at dawn);
                    and then nothing, just so, matters;
(after dinner, goodnight, good morning, in the kitchen, at dawn);
and then: I'm tired of explaining, then, of justifying (justifying myself);
        (and I wanted
to say, just that: of justifying myself—as I explained—'forever');
                            and then:
tired of such an insistent recourse; (ghosts); (saying: because you will
have noticed how I have rushed, insistent, to have recourse . . . ;
and so on; (to ghosts);
             but calmly, Luciana, really (30th
September), later; but then I want to say, now: 'forever' (...):

so, here (in Cerisy); (so they were saying): we have, here, a chinaman
(and the chinaman is me, naturally);
                    on the motorway I was explaining, too,
the counterattack on the literary operation, radically, immediate (and
so on); and we spoke of triumphant opportunism, too (and when I said,
    then,
reformism, in fact, I wanted really to say opportunism, instead);
                                            because
the chinese position (I said) justifies every hope (and it's not a question
of working-class elite, in short, but the end of prehistory, truly,
and so on);
            and to my wife I spoke of the quantity of unhappiness,
        meanwhile (of the
quality; and so on);
        I wanted to say: it justifies us too; and also our children;
and I wanted to say: it justifies the moment of utopia (but really, but
        for us, too,
but here, now): this moment (justifies);
                            and I wanted to say: forever;
(but in the night bar, in Palermo, I heard them really, saying: why
do you live, you? and they were saying: how do you justify yourself?
                                            saying:
        but do you justify yourself?)
but now, you see: but now, what tiredness? and what (in this our
prehistory), what calm?
                but you see the mud which is at our backs,
and the sun among the trees, and the children who sleep:
                                        the children
who dream (who speak, dreaming); (but the children, you see them, so
        restless);
(sleeping, the children); (dreaming, now):

Antônio Moura   *Translated from Portuguese by Stefan Tobler*

Father

> *This is because the species,*
> *in which lies the germ of our being,*
> *has a nearer and prior claim upon us than the individual.*
> Arthur Schopenhauer

Your hand foam undone in the sand
Your ear conch at the bottom of the sea
Drums of your temples and your hips
beating on the day when you centaur
galloped, galloped, galloped
over the fire-tattooed rose of my mother's womb,
de-petalling her
When I called you from the depths of a shadow
and you naively, unknowingly, looked for me
with howls and eyes possessed by the secret daemon
that smashes into everything in its intent
to bring, through a gust, a wind,
a being to drift blindly among the blind
in a maze of echoes and secret signs
where at any moment—by a gust,
a wind—it can be undone
Dad, nothing for it but for both
to hold out a hand in forgiveness, faced
with nature's indecipherable purposes:
You, for, unwittingly, making me
enter time, without support or hold,
I for making you, without choice, my instrument

Walking home, usual routine,
on your brow the daily sweat

for a loaf of bread, stars
above, remains of the dead

below your feet that walk
carefully to not disturb them,

the wind brushes your forehead and time
treads your temples, horse's hooves

drag love's flowers off at a gallop
to another road, not this one

that you come up every day, among
strange faces—one is of someone

who didn't come—, you sense the smell
of the shadows of people who passed

and disappeared a corner earlier,
who your eyes won't ever meet.

Oh, yes, miniature existence,
this little walk every day

as you return, antônio and nocturnal
to your home, miniature of another home

—whole, universe, that waits behind night

Notes on Contributors

Melih Cevdet Anday (1915–2002) was born and lived in Istanbul, where he worked as a journalist and teacher. A novelist, playwright and essayist, as well as a poet, he was a leading member of the *Garip* movement.

Özdemir Asaf (1923–1981) was born in Ankara, but spent most of his life in Istanbul. During his lifetime Asaf won substantial critical acclaim and earned a large readership; since his death his reputation and his readership have continued to grow.

Michael Ayres is the author of three collections, the most recent of which is *Kinetic* (Shearsman Books, 2007).

K.C. Clapham is from Lytham St Annes, Lancashire. She now lives in London where she is a part-time student on the Poetic Practice MA at Royal Holloway University of London, and the full-time production editor at *The Journal of Bone and Joint Surgery*. Her work has also appeared in *How2*.

Kelvin Corcoran's most recent collection is *Backward Turning Sea* (Shearsman Books, 2008). He lives in Cheltenham.

Sarah Anne Cox is the author of *Arrival* (Krupskaya 2002) and *Parcel* (O Books 2006). She lives in San Francisco where she teaches, windsurfs and cares for her two children.

Jen Crawford's collection *Bad Appendix* was published by Titus Books in 2008. She teaches creative writing at the University of Auckland, New Zealand, and has a PhD in Creative Arts from the University of Wollongong, Australia.

Óscar Curieses was born in Madrid in 1972. The poems here come from his recent collection *Sonetos del útero* (*Sonnets from the Womb*, Bartleby Eds, 2007).

Valentino Gianuzzi lives in Lima. A scholar, translator and editor, he co-translated the complete poems of Vallejo with Michael Smith for Shearsman.

Catherine Hales lives in Berlin, where she works as a freelance translator.

Lynne Hjelmgaard was born in New York, but now lives in Copenhagen. Redbeck Press of Bristol published her *Manhattan Sonnets* in 2003.

Norbert Hummelt lives in Berlin. The poems here are drawn from his collection *Totentanz* (Luchterhand Literaturverlag, Munich, 2007). Also well-known as a translator, his most recent publication is a new version of Eliot's *The Waste Land*.

Hendrik Jackson lives in Berlin. The poems here are drawn from his most recent collection *Dunkelströme* (kookbooks, Idstein, 2006). Also available from the same publisher are his essays, *Im Innern der zerbrechenden Schale* (2007).

Norman Jope lives in Plymouth. His publications include *For the Wedding Guest* (Stride, 1997), *The Book of Bells and Candles* (Waterloo Press, 2009) and, as editor, the anthology *In the Presence of Sharks* (Phlebas Press, 2007).

HELEN LOPEZ lives in Anglesey, and is widely-exhibited painter. Her first collection will be published by Shearsman Books in late 2009.

GEORGE MESSO's new collection *Hearing Still* is due from Shearsman in June.

ANTÔNIO MOURA was born in Belém, at the mouth of the Amazon. His publications include: *Dez* (1996), *Hong Kong & outros poemas* (1999), *Rio Silêncio* (2004) and also translations of Rabearivelo and Vallejo.

ALASDAIR PATERSON lives in Exeter. Collections of his work were published by Pig Press in the 1980s, including *Floating World, Selected Poems 1973–1982*.

NICK POTAMITIS has taught Film Studies at various institutions and writes on the history of Greek cinema. His publications include *N.* (Perdika Press, 2006).

ANNA RECKIN's poetry and essays have been published in the UK and the USA. She now lives in Norwich, and is working on a book about landscape and contemporary experimental Anglophone poetry.

PETER ROBINSON is the author of *The Look of Goodbye* and *Talk About Poetry* (both from Shearsman Books) as well as a number of collections from Carcanet, including a *Selected Poems*. He is a Professor at the University of Reading.

ROBERT SAXTON is editorial director of an illustrated book publishing company. His three collections are *The Promise Clinic, Manganese* and *Local Honey*.

IAN SEED edits the online journal *Shadowtrain*; his first collection, *Anonymous Intruder*, was published by Shearsman Books in January 2009.

EDOARDO SANGUINETI was born in Genoa in 1930. His first collection, *Laborintus*, was published in 1956. In the early 1960s, he played a major role in the *Novissimi* group and in the 'neo-avantgarde' *Gruppo 63*. His poetry is collected in *Segnalibro (1951–1981)* and in *Il gatto lupesco (1982–2001)*.

STEVE SPENCE lives in Plymouth. His poetry and reviews have appeared in *Tears in the Fence, Magma, Stand, Fire, Great Works* and many other UK journals.

NATHAN THOMPSON's first collection, *the arboretum towards the beginning*, was published by Shearsman Books in 2008. He lives at present in Jersey.

STEFAN TOBLER is a freelance translator from Portuguese and German. His translation of Roger Willemsen's *Afghan Journey* was a 2007 Recommended Translation from English PEN. His translations of Antônio Moura were recently awarded a commendation in the 2008 BCLA Dryden Translation Prize.

ALAN WALL published two collections with Shearsman in 2008: *Alexander Pope at Twickenham* and *Gilgamesh*. Also in 2008 he published his sixth novel, *Sylvie's Riddle* (Quartet Books, London). He is Professor of Creative Writing at the University of Chester.

TONY WILLIAMS has a collection forthcoming from Salt Publishing.

Printed in the United Kingdom by
Lightning Source UK Ltd., Milton Keynes
138452UK00001B/37/P